35 AMAZING GROUP ACTIVITIES

The Evolution of Student Behavior

—∽—

A Study of Group Activities That Work in Schools

- Something Positive • How I See Myself • Let's Talk to Parents
- Let's Talk Positive and Negative • Do You Know Who You Are? • The Audition
- Let's Talk Self-Esteem • Self Image • Let's Make a Decision
- Understanding Our Values • Clarifying Our Values and Feelings
- Are You Aggressive, Passive, or Assertive? • Self Awareness and Goals
- Let's Play a Game • Let's Talk the Right Way
- Lower Your Tone • Let's Have a Debate • Are We Agreeing or Not?
- Do You Have Goals? • Body Images • Let's Identify Your Positive Personal Traits
- Are We All Grown Up? • What Is the Impression of Yourself?
- Personal Strengths • What Is in that Grab Bag? • Let's Talk Different Families
- Let's Rationalize a Situation • Your School
- Choosing Your Behavior • Let's Discuss Gender • Body Images Through the Media • Alcoholism in Families • Teen Moms Talk • Positive Solutions
- Positive Consequences • Let's Text

RICH ESPOSITO, M.S.

outskirts
press

Outskirts Press, Inc.
http://www.outskirtspress.com

ISBN: 978-1-4787-7219-4

Outskirts Press and the "OP" logo are trademarks belonging to Outskirts Press, Inc.

PRINTED IN THE UNITED STATES OF AMERICA

This book is dedicated to all the diverse students who will benefit from these group intervention activities. It has been evidence based that students who are involved in-group work will improve their life and academics. These activities are proven success for each student, who participates and is committed to move forward in their lives.

Doug

Thanks for the Inspiration!!

Rich Espon

Table of Contents

Acknowledgements

A number of people have contributed to the foundation of creating this book for individuals who are helping students succeed in life.

It is important to acknowledge parents, especially my father who continues to inspire me with drive, determination, and intelligence. Always listening to my mother's words of wisdom. All of the students who worked with me during these group activities, clients, Gary Edwards, Barry Selman, Peter Klueber, counselors, teachers, and all the educational workers who read and used the amazing successful activities in this book.

I hope all the amazing topics in this book that helped students move forward with their life and academics, inspire you to continue the passion to support students who are suffering emotionally, socially, and academically. I hope all these amazing topics create exciting inspiration with the students who are always looking to learn, and find new ways to survive in a different code of behavior.

Special thanks to my family for understanding when I am working with clients during my private practice; they respect the fact it needs to be quiet.

Authors Notes

This book is not a biology or science book. However, you will find brief discussions that only surface about evolution, biology, and the anatomy of human life. Unlike any other activity book, I describe and capture the science and evolution of student behavior, so you can see what the students are feeling, as they go through some serious psychological concerns during their childhood, and adolescence years.

The Beginning

Perhaps you feel fearful of the judgment of your colleagues? You are stressed out after you were not able to control your school group activity session? You are getting frazzled, and feel uncertain what the next group activity or 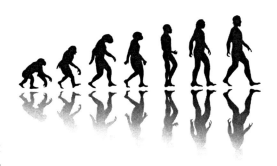 lesson would be like? At times, you may have a conflict with the administrators taking your advice on student behavior. You suddenly start to feel guilty because you have the passion to do well, help solve student complications, and teach for every student. Several of your colleagues have noticed you seem to be a bit frustrated, and tense. The students show no respect to you for there is no leadership in your group work or have any amazing group activity topics to keep the students intrigued? I know how you feel. I was there!

If educational professionals, typically guidance counselors and social workers, can pull together and get a better understanding and reference of the students childhood struggles of living through poverty, adversity and change, it would create a better learning environment. In addition, the counselors, teachers, educators, interns, parents, and mentors who are all looking to challenge themselves with the anxiety of dealing with all the educational differences, frustrations, and students' emotional circumstances, as a professional will find a less stress free environment.

As a professional school counselor we are obligated to serve all students with leadership, advocacy, accountability, and provide a safe learning environment. I have collected data and evidence based results in group work, finding that the tough and unstable community environment for students to live in can create biological life changing circumstances, thus, diminishing student performance. Today we know by nature humans are highly social animals, therefore, when we see a change in behavior, it is then evident that a change of behavior is learned in our harsh society. A tough irrational society is impacting students intellectually, failing them to achieve academically as well as behaving in the classroom setting. Most important, with all the severe changes in humanity, culture, and the crime in the environment, it is altering a shift in a child's biological development process. The evolution and growth of student behavior is damaged because of the lack of control and the lack of predictability involving social and psychological processes related to the environment the students are raised in. The fast changing of time becomes a struggle to adapt for youngsters. Major environmental predictors, such as fear, stress, and over populated neighborhoods affect our brain chemistry. The constant change in the environment has been a plague-ridden syndrome for over 65 million years. The human immune system is distressed during rapid changes and it doesn't work as healthy as it needs to be. Through all the psychological strain of adapting in society and the environment, many students today are developing high blood pressure, increased heart rate, continuous worry, and social anxiety. Clearly, these are just a few biological indicators for clinical depression, anxiety, and eventually a deteriorating health.

Students are suffering emotionally, socially, and academically, and of more than 17 years spent working in New York City Schools; having meetings with school psychologists, counselors, teachers, and social workers I have assessed that students need critical intellectual tools. Group activities are perfect for school counselors to help improve student development in social skills, expressing feelings, communication, and personal growth. The research and data I have conducted tells us these amazing activities are helping students improve socially, emotionally, and academically. Students need a way to relieve the stress, if there is no activity in their lives. I have found students are struggling to deal with the harsh realities that are much damaging to them. Mental stresses are developing in their body; endorphins (Neurotransmitters in the brain to relieve pain) are filling up and suppressing mood conditions, anger, frustrations, anxiety and many more internal pain illnesses that are not being released, hurting youngsters within. The students need to release endorphins filling with unhealthy conditions. I find students are releasing their endorphins in a very unhealthy cruel aggressive behavior. Students need to find a healthy release of endorphins, like exercise, social interaction, and extracurricular activities. The brain is creating uncertainty, doubt, and progression as they grow in our tough society and environment.

THE REASON FOR THIS BOOK

The subject of my book is to briefly clarify the meaning of student behavior through scientific research on primate-based evidence (Baboons) by Dr. Robert Sapolsky.

Sapolsky who revealed and studied many behaviors from primates closely resemble those of humans. Like us, primates have developed large brains to navigate the complexities of large societies. How did primates survive? How do we survive? Sometimes it makes me feel that it is a miracle that any of us survived. However, bottom line, if we are able to adapt in society and the environment, then we survive. If we were not able to adapt and create problems, then we would die off.

Studies show if there is a change in any form of anatomy, and behavior which has been altered because of the environment and society changing. Human life will be vulnerable and at a threat to survive. That brings me to my collection of activities. The activities help reshape behavior so students who are struggling in the environment, whether it is aggressive or passive will definitely be part of a success story.

I strongly focus on my data evidence based group activities that work for students who are struggling in a poverty societal enclave. In the suburban communities they are confronted with major bullying, heroin, cocaine, including other major drugs that are killing kids with psychological side effects, overdose, brain impairment and a historical amount of teenage suicide.

What makes us to really survive in society? Are we surviving because we are ranked on top in our human hierarchy system? Are we surviving because of our friends and family helping us? Are we surviving because we let our anger and endorphins out on others? Are we surviving because we interact with others and try our hardest to be accepted? I took into consideration my training, data, study and collecting of some amazing group activities that evidently will help shape young minds to endure the challenges they are confronted with. I was determined and set out to assess the causes that are affecting student struggles, which is the reason for this book.

Group activities are perfect to help young minds explore interaction, build stronger self-esteem, build social confidence, and to have a better understanding of their place in society. The data and evidence based group activities I have collected is to help overcome the student problems, adaption and change during their developmental process that might have been effected through society, parents, and peer pressure. The activities also help teaching and group counseling, making it easier for educational professions. Most important, the students will enjoy learning, feel inspired, and finding themselves motivated to come to school. For those of us who are struggling with the student behavioral issues and find that it becomes difficult to reach, inspire, and motivate the children will have clear expectations and consistent results through these amazing group activities.

Below you will find a sample graph of evidence based group activities. You will find student improvement in English. The sample graph contains 75 cohort boy and girl students that represent a diverse ethnic background of African Americans, Hispanic American, White American, and other groups who were not on track for graduation. Reminder, the cohort included 10 special education students. The student age group ranges from 15-17 years. There were 7 groups each meeting once a week. Each group contained 10 students per group. There were an equal amount of boys and girls per group. Each activity I have used is the top 35 amazing group activities. The first sample group evidence subject is English. You will find for the first marking grade period, 9.1 percent of my English students were failing. 72.7 percent were passing. 18.2 percent were on the honor roll. In the Second marking grade period it remained the same. Consistent weekly group sessions continued with the activities. Look at the third marking period, you will find an increase of 9.1 percent. 81 percent of the students have passed with no failures.

The second sample graph is using amazing group activities that improved students academically who were in all major science subjects, Living environment, Earth Science, and Chemistry (Not including Physics). The sample contains 75 cohort boy and girl students in a diverse ethnic background. Same as above, the student age group ranges from 15-17 years. You will find for the first grade period, 42.9 percent were failing all three-science subjects. 57.1 percent were passing. In the second marking grade period failures decreased from 42.9 percent to 28.6 percent a reduction of 14.3 percent. What is outstanding, the increase of 57.1 percent passing increased to 71.4 percent. Amazingly, look at the third marking grade period, another decrease in failures from 28.6 percent to 14.3 percent. The passing percentage remained the same, however, astonishingly; there was an improved passing percentage with a 14.3 percent honor roll percentage. The results are clear evidence that my activities help young students today to improve themselves socially, emotionally, and academically with consistent and weekly groups.

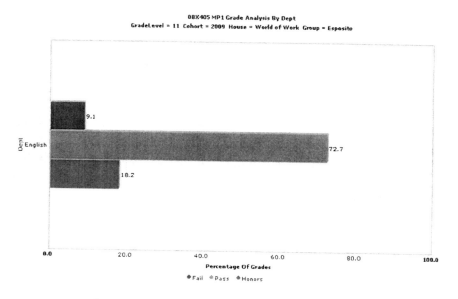

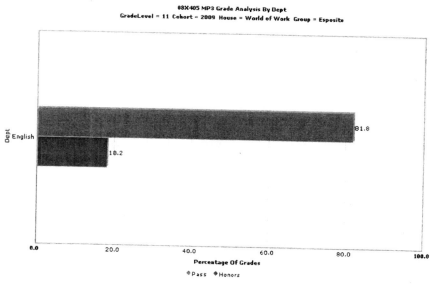

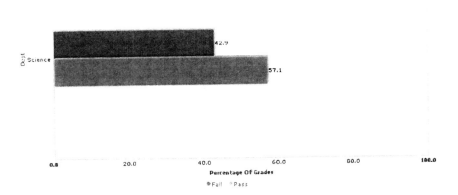

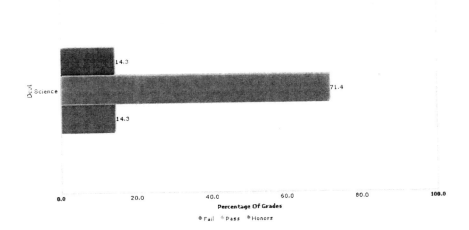

The data is considered to have outstanding reliability with consistency using the activities. Students have improved their verbal comprehension and vocabulary; emotionally students have shown an increase by interacting with their peers, adults, and teachers. Writing skills have also shown a major increase, cultural understanding, self-awareness, positive attitude, better strategies for thinking, and most important improvement in academics.

I find in my assessment, student's distressed behavior is evolving around the people and the environment they are surrounded by. Young students are influenced and conditioned very easily by hoodlums who are controlling the neighborhoods. Later, I describe the manipulation coming from the neighborhoods and environment that are severely affecting the evolution of student behavior, creating major concerns physically and psychologically. Young students who are starting to take their first steps on the road to be productive human beings are absent-minded living in a society that can destroy their humanity.

While gathering my data, I have constructed and modified amazing group activities leading students to create stronger thought, developing better interaction and communication. Students have developed a positive attitude, and a healthier outlook on education. The evidence also indicated students are thinking about a positive future. The activities help recondition student behavior that are impaired developmentally in a controlled society that is stimulated by an evolutionary force of demands. Children of all ages, race, and ethnic backgrounds are facing major issues in a diseased society, whether it's urban or suburban. A distressed childhood that plagues us with troubled and extreme emotional disturbances will affect all of us. One way or another, concerned parents, education and job related issues are affected.

POVERTY LEVEL

The poverty level continues to grow. I have researched there are over 22 million United States children living in poverty. The children raised in a socially and emotionally negative environment are much less likely to have their needs met. The children who are trapped in an unhealthy society are impacted emotionally and subject to serious consequences of biological change in the brain, skewing their understanding of being successful. Students are delayed and obstructed in their development of maturity and the overall achievement academically. In fact, I find many ghoulish neighborhood food marts to provide unhealthy nutritional products. I have assessed, before any students are able to  find a quality super market, or organic fruit marts, they will pass by several unhealthy fast food joints, like Kentucky fried chicken, McDonald's, Burger King, and Wendy's. To make matters worse, students will walk by liquor and cigarette stores on every corner, selling to minors. The unhealthy approach is immediately influencing students that drinking, smoking and eating fast food is perfectly fine. In fact, the urban bodega stores smell like roach powder, and kids are spending money they don't have on unnatural high calorie food. Certainly, unhealthy and contaminated circumstances in the environment are clear indications of obesity, asthma, and lack of nourishment. In my assessment as I work with students from all over the states and cities, I have found kids in New York City schools are faced with living in poor neighborhoods, poor social structure, heavy demands, and unnatural environmental conditions. The structure of the environment and the neighborhoods are set up for failure. The kids will fall into societal deceptions. Students learn that they find less time for discovery, less time for innovation, and less time for invention. Many emotional suffering students are unconsiously not focused because of the brain chemistry that is conditioned and staggered with corruption, illegal behavior, and hostility. The students mixed feelings condition them to live with the mindset of always struggling to survive with difficulty and trouble.

Let's Briefly Talk Evolutionary Psychology

So, I briefly described why students are underachieving because of the rapid changes and the environmental disparities. The fast change in society leads us to the disruption of human evolution, and the affects it can have when trying to adapt, and the struggle for students to keep up. In addition, I have given you clear evidence and measure on student improvement, and the positive effects of student behavior during the process of my group activities.

Today, we don't hear or talk about human evolutionary psychology so much. Evolutionary psychology is simply, why humans act the way they do? Again, simply because of the environmental changes which alters the brain chemistry and adaption to the fast changing environment (John Hopkins School of Education, Bennett, Huebel and Wiesel, 1965). I do not want to spend much time on evolutionary psychology, but it is becoming a rising issue why humans, especially the young, are struggling to adapt to change, affecting their future potential.

For years, many of the group activity books have led us professional's right to the core of activities. The activities are not quite evident they work for students, and educators are like; let's have fun blah, blah, blah. Most of the activity books are wrong when it comes to helping children develop stronger intellectually. However, let's not eliminate the fun from the activities offered. I find that it is important to understand the evolution of student behavior before we work as counselors in helping students succeed through group activities.

Let's look at a common dysfunction in evolutionary psychology. We need to look at another dynamic to see the individual difference in behavior and the psychological patterns in how student bodies are working. The feeling of being isolated, lonely, and depressed are because of the struggling adaption of one's certain environmental situation. The alteration of being cognitively passive to others who force demands is a change in the brain chemistry. The shift of thought from the force of demands skews the natural and normal behavior of human development. Students are eventually adapted to demands when the brain is distorted or mislead, therefore, the structure and nature of the mental mechanism will operate differently and not biologically natural when affected by the environmental demands. (Bechtel & McCauley, 1999; Bechtel, 2001).

A struggle to adapt in a negative environment upbringing distresses the special learning mechanisms in the brain. That brings us to understand when an individual is emotionally impaired psychologically there is a malfunction in the thought process. The facts indicate through research, The National Institute of Neurological Disorders state the behavior patterns are altered and individuals are subject to stress, high blood pressure, and problems with concentration. Students will then ignore education, disregard their academics, neglect any form of learning and the motivation to perform scholastically. The evolution of student behavior is distorted because of the rapid social environmental changes and its demands, straining students to think positive. When we have students acting out, we now know that there are reasons for us educators to explore what is behind their acting out before we concern ourselves with anxiety or worry that we are doing something wrong as educators.

Dr. Robert Sapolsky, professor of neuroscience at Stanford University and a research associate with the Institute of Primate Research show that data clearly indicates primates have a greater mortality rate when they are isolated from society or their ranks in the hierarchy structure. Sapolsky gave incredible evidence on primates (baboons) who have fewer social interactions will develop diseases. He has also found infectious diseases get worse when primates are caught in a social hierarchy that abandons them.

In comparison, now let's look at us humans. You can show the same results with human life. Although not as simple in human psychological study, humans have a shorter life expectancy when stuffed with isolation from society. We now know a person is more immune to infectious diseases when fear and stuffing their feelings causes unhealthy thoughts and behavior. The serious research shows both sexes and different cultures are impacted psychologically. In fact, what is even more astounding, the impact is as large and serious as the epidemic of cigarette smoking, obesity, and lack of physical activity. If we think about the survival of the fittest, in essence, the students are struggling to survive, but are barely finishing. Can we understand the student struggles to survive in a complex evolutionary society? Or are the students crying silently for help depending on our efforts to help them survive?

We are born as social beings. Students are living in social groups that require major demands and influences from society. To not be able to develop socially, something tells us there has been a disturbance psychologically? Adapting easily like animals, students are faced and challenged socially, emotionally, and academically. In the urban toxic communities, students are faced with danger every day. It is a brutal struggle. Let's think for a moment? Some students are starving, committing crime, dying of disease and drugs because of the overcrowding population.

I like to continue my evidence using my childhood science fair project; I could remember as a 12-year-old kid breeding mice to participate in a science fair. Inside of a 10 gallon fish tank, I had two pedigree homegrown white mice. After several weeks, I eventually had five mice. I continued the breeding and it doubled to ten mice. One morning, my brother and I went down stairs and found several mice had died or were killed. Three variations occurred, one, the tank was over populated, and they started to kill each other. Two, it became territorial inside of the tank. Finally, the dominant mouse would have most of the food, and controlled most of the females inside of the tank. I have found there were no dominant female mice.

In comparison, the neighborhoods are over populated, aggression occurs in many communities, which are an evolutionary feature that is troubling students today. Students are being exploited by dominant people and pushed into oppressed situations. Just like the mice, vulnerable students are not able to protect themselves. They are being pushed into drugs or influenced to commit some petty crime, get forced into joining gangs, and there are some grave situations as well.

They are not being supported by low income parents who are struggling themselves. Children are being born from wed-lock, have no father or mother, and eventually are raised by their grandparents. Certainly low self-esteem can develop when children are not motivated or brought up in confident family values. So can we understand the rapid changes and disturbances of child development? Can we help children who are faced with the human evolution of social change and its harsh society?

Let's look at our stressful Hierarchy System

Clearly, individuals who are submissive it is more likely they will be part of a low ranking hierarchy system. Researchers have found

MASLOW'S HIERARCHY OF NEEDS

AH-HA!
SELF-ACTUALIZATION
/ ESTEEM NEEDS
& Belongingness
Love Needs   GO TEAM!
SAFETY NEEDS
STABILITY...
BIOLOGICAL &
PSYCHOLOGICAL
NEEDS

a massive amount of stress, high blood pressure, elevated level of stress hormones, a reproductive system is unregulated and psychological strain is conditioning students to behave irrational. So, we are strongly faced with a damaged hierarchy system in our modern American society, communities, and neighborhoods. Living in a directive demanding society is generating toxic stress for our children. Students are pressured and strained to live in a constant world of worry, instability, and threat through intimidation, imperfections and controlled neighborhoods. Students need to feel safety, stability, loved, belongingness, and self-actualization. These main ingredients will build and help any weak self-esteem biological curve.

Like no other group activity book, it is important for you to vision and understand the concept of human behavior in its context first and its early evolution of human development. It is important that we accept and appreciate the scientific study in human stress, poverty and the human hierarchy system. If we can develop a stronger vision and understanding of student suffering, we can generate better teaching and develop accomplishing students academically. Students are suffering scholastically when exposed to early stress. Early exposure to unhealthy situations is severely impacting students to fail psychologically, and academically.

Accumulated Data

In this book you will find 35 amazing group activities that work in schools. My data and evidence based material is an accumulated student portfolio. According to the American School Counselor Association, school counselors accountability is to gather important data from their pupil personnel meetings, and most important their own observation on students behavior. The collecting of teacher observations, parent discussions, attendance, student interaction, home visits, discipline, grade assessments, and drug abuse are much needed material and evidence to package your portfolio on each student.

Building a mental health folder on each student will help you develop a vision, statistics, and verification of each student's success and personal/social development. Academic support and group work with your peers will help most students who are truant, who are failing, lost in transition, have no social skills, have no communication with their parents, or have irrational behavioral issues. The understanding of the student development will help shape their character in society, as opposed to the learned behavior in their troubled communities, or home life that might be in disarray.

As a school counselor, in my observation, I have found that students went from failing to passing during my group activities. As indicated in the graphs, some students have gained honor roll status, participated in building school community, have become leaders as well as professional athletes. In fact, I have graduated two professional athletes, most recent in TJ Rivera (New York Mets, 2016), using my amazing group activities. Students who get involved in-group activities have found themselves to get in touch with their feelings and emotions. There has been a growing number of students expressing themselves and communicating more with their peers. They found themselves to socialize more, and not isolating themselves from society. The group activities allow the students to truly step out of their shadow, that they have been hiding behind for who knows how long? Students have later given the indication to get involved socially interacting in after school activities like a chess club, Friday groups, or even just being part of a mandated counseling session. Students have shown increased understanding, cultivating better learning and development. In fact, their moral understanding has even developed stronger building better communication with friends, eliminating peer pressure, improving their unstable living conditions or just being able to connect with their parents.

KILLER TOXINS

This book actually came about in essence of understanding the evolution of student behavior, struggles, and their challenges of everyday life. Students would express themselves in many different ways. Some students were aggressive, and some were passive. I have assessed, most students act out aggressively and violently. Group counseling activities are a critical need because of the low motivation and high poverty circumstances that is taken over their humanity and natural biological development. My data meets the distinctive needs for counselors who are helping and assisting students who are struggling with early life problems. The activities help student's irrational and unproductive behavior in a school setting.

Let's face it; in high poverty neighborhoods you will find rat-infested areas. Astonishingly, I have seen creepy larger fuzzy water rat's unusually chasing smaller cats on polluted streets. A study by Columbia University Public Health Department finds there is an infestation of eerie roaches in urban areas creating community asthma within the young. At times, you can see water bugs flying from one building to another. You might find gloomy prostitution on dark corners, asking to exchange sex for money. The heavy drugs and crime are some of the variables of toxins as kids walk through these threatening areas every day. We know these harmful impurities will inhibit the production of new brain cells among our newborn and adolescent children. Let's not forget the suburban areas' that are settling with troops of drug lords who quietly live in the dark shadows controlling the streets with heroin and other death related drugs. In the northern suburbs and rural areas, there is an epidemic of heroin. There has been an increase with students overdosing on heroin. I understand the student's behavior, environment, and pressure that they are going through, and this has enabled me to relate and professionally interact with the students and their difficult journey to educational achievement and success.

A safe healthy environment

I had the chance to grow up in a typical middle class neighborhood in the northern Bronx, New York. Today it is a changed place I think about as a true survival playground. Although the northern Bronx was faced with low economic growth, it was still cleaned up through neighborhood community watch and tough neighborhood personalities that kept away outcast tyrants or heavy drug lords that tried to invade new areas and create new territories for their drug controls. I was able to attend a newly zoned high school that was for the neighborhood students and community. Traditionally in the 1970's, my friends and I would play whiffle ball, a game with a plastic baseball bat and a plastic ball on the street corner of our block, as well as the famous stickball. Later, we would all hear and listen to every ones mother screaming out the window at 6:00pm for dinnertime. As we ran home for dinner to sit around the table and feast with our family, we would later return at the corner for some kick the can, or hide and seek. Traditionally, during the summer, we would have the annual 4th of July vibrant block parties without shootouts, and later before the nighttime firework celebration, all of us friends would run to the park for some sandlot baseball to then only watch the fireworks burst with color as we hit baseballs in the sky. We evolved in a community where there was not much crime, some occasional street fights, we had races around the corner, played skelly with bottle caps filled with wax, even hop scotch with the girls. However, we still managed safely to stay out on chilly school nights, and then run home to have homemade warm chocolate chip cookies and milk to watch the Charlie Brown family holiday seasonal episodes starting at 8pm. We all knew each other with a warm bond, and we would walk to school together, do homework together and at times some of our parents would drive us to school. It was a community that made us feel safe, warm, and friendly.

Unhealthy Change

Today, our old traditional northern neighborhood became a tribal ghetto; The low white picket fences are now 6 or even 8 foot iron barriers with triple locks, the neighborhood deli became a group Jehovah Witness Club, and neglected trash is gathering in a pile on the corner where we would play our whiffle ball games.

Many inner city schools are accepting students with different issues from Brooklyn, Queens, and the rest of the five-boros'. The neighborhoods are being overturned with violent kids from different cultures and third world countries. New generations of diversity are flooding into neighborhoods and communities with their different psychology, bringing in different beliefs, religion and values. Our neighborhood homes have transformed into prison-like buildings with residential window guards, left over eaten chicken bones on the side curb, even ten-foot gold looking iron fences surrounding my grandfather's old red brick house with his tomato garden destroyed, his nurtured fruit trees, and his unattended well harvested grapevine which doesn't exist anymore. I remember the house visiting baby doctor; he packed his bags to find a safer environment, a new home and a new office.

The traditional Norman Rockwell neighborhoods are all gone. The aroma of homemade cookies, and Italian gravy turned into a polluted chemical of gasoline, burned tires and low flame fires burning in steel barrels at the corner of our neighborhood park.

During my high school years, my memories of being part of a healthy community was something I never thought would end, I was able to run to the corner deli and buy a homemade Italian ice, write for the school paper, I played for a high school basketball team and I always tried to just be part of school trips to the Museum of Natural History in Manhattan, where I would spend hours fantasizing about living in the era of Sigmund Freud, Carl Young, Eric Ericson, and one of the longest living text book psychiatrist's, Dr. Albert Ellis.

I believe that everyone can benefit from these amazing group activities and can be excited and confident by the data on which they are based. It is important for a new counselor, teacher, or parent to envision the mind of a young boy or girl going to school. We seem to forget the trials and tribulations children are encountering during their childhood years. Most children in poverty are conditioned and immune to live in an unhealthy society. I have reviewed the scientific facts that living in a hierarchy culture will develop your personality, and shape your behavior, (Robert Sapolsky, 1985) and for this result, I decided strongly to go even further to pursue group activities and modify the activities around student behavior and their struggles in a poverty environment. I have found that struggling students need to be reshaped, re-conditioned, and re-structured so their behavior is to not think about negativity or disparities. I have found that research tells us that 70% of student's behavioral issues are formed in the environment they live in (The American School Counseling Association). How are kids going to change? A teacher in the classroom is teaching their subject, not teaching psychological balance for students to adapt in their communities. The accountability is up to school counseling or any other mental health professional's effort to work with children who are affected by the human evolutionary change. I found that the group work is better than individual work for there is much of a social learning structure to help students interact with their peers. Each group of students that participate in these amazing activities or other group organized sessions will find that they can support each other. In fact, make new friends as well. They find that helping someone who might be suffering from the hierarchy world or other life struggling circumstances is rewarding.

I decided to bring together the best-structured group activities to help students thrive and reach their goals. It was a fascinating learning experience for me to see students interact diligently and succeed after a well-designed and organized group activity that worked during my practice as a counselor. My findings and data are results that changed students' behavior emotionally, socially, and academically after three grading marking periods.

Below I have additional evidence to support students who are struggling in their overall psychological abilities to educate themselves, and improve their comprehensive thinking of values, beliefs, and self-confidence to move forward.

The following graph indicates additional clear evidence base material in student success. In the first marking grade period, in the math subject you will find 33.3 percent of the 75 cohort diverse students were failing. In addition, you will find 50.0 percent were passing, 8.3 percent were truant and 8.3 percent were missing projects. In the second marking grade period, you will see a decrease in failures at 25.0 percent, and an increase of passing at 66.7 percent. The 8.3 percent of students who were missing projects completed the math work with other student's in-group session dropping that percentage to zero (0). Finally, in the third marking grade period you will see another decrease in math failure dropping down to 16.7 percent, and the passing rate increasing to 75.0 percent.

In social studies, the first marking grad period you can see 20.0 percent were failing, 60.0 percent were passing and 10.0 percent were honors. The other 10.0 percent are missing projects. In the second marking grade period, it all remained the same.

Once again, staying consistent with the group activities, the third marking grade period shows a major increase in passing at 80.0 percent. You will see a decrease in failures at 10.0 percent; projects were completed in-group activity sessions leaving that percentage at zero (0) and the honors remaining at 10.0 percent. I can assess that all of these activities are clear indications of better comprehensive thinking, stronger values, beliefs, and stronger self-confidence. The students expressed themselves with amazing overall psychological improvement.

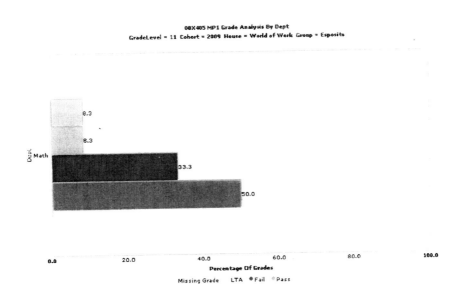

08X405 MP1 Grade Analysis By Dept
GradeLevel = 11 Cohort = 2009 House = World of Work Group = Esposito

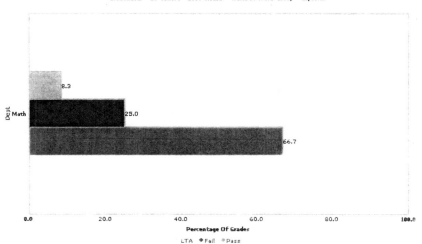

08X405 MP2 Grade Analysis By Dept
GradeLevel = 11 Cohort = 2009 House = World of Work Group = Esposito

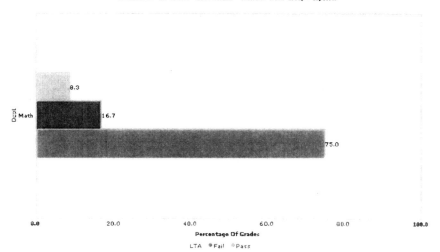

08X405 MP3 Grade Analysis By Dept
GradeLevel = 11 Cohort = 2009 House = World of Work Group = Esposito

08X405 MP1 Grade Analysis By Dept
GradeLevel = 11 Cohort = 2009 House = World of Work Group = Esposito

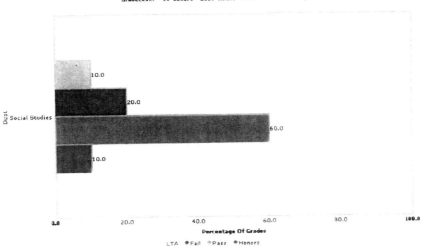

08X405 MP3 Grade Analysis By Dept
GradeLevel = 11 Cohort = 2009 House = World of Work Group = Esposito

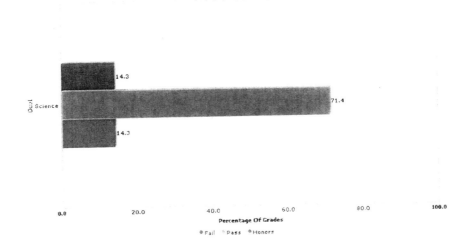

The beginning of my amazing group activities were structured and modified around the theory of Rational Emotive Behavioral Therapy:

Since my freshman year in high school, I was able to take a psychology class and immediately became interested in the study of human behavior, change, research, treatment, and counseling therapy. I was fascinated with the facts of why people were behaving irrational. I later joined an after school psychology club, and eventually became president of a psychology society at Lehman College, in the Bronx, New York. I was part of organized trips to the world famous Bronx Zoo as I observed animals behind the scenes that suffered injury. In fact, I would experience animals crying, and suffering as I observed behind the scenes. Some animals would get upset because they did not want to be in certain cages or playgrounds. They would throw tantrums, biting cages, or ranting back and forth.

I also always loved attending the Natural History Museum in New York, the Holocaust Museum, and the National Geographic Museum in Washington D.C. All of these trips were fascinating, allowing me to review character, behavior, and human interaction.

It wasn't until after my first year at Purchase College I wanted to learn more about Rational Emotive Behavior Therapy. I attended some required workshops at the Albert Ellis Institute and was drawn in with the treatment technique in Rational Emotive Behavior Therapy (REBT).

It was on a beautiful hot summer breeze in July 2000, when I had my first meeting and training with Dr. Albert Ellis in his brownstone, New York City office. I knew I wanted to look deeper into culture, society, and the demands that changed behavior. Ellis is the founder of Rational Emotive Behavior Therapy (REBT). Later, I became a serious counseling student at Long Island University, preparing myself strongly knowing that my chosen profession was to be a psychotherapist, a counselor, a psychologist, a life coach, or some other mental health specialist. I have read and studied about Dr. Ellis in my course work and studies at Purchase College. I had some amazing professors that inspired me to continue to move forward with my passion to study human behavior and counseling on the graduate level. My factual graphs and data uncover results that group work using the Rational Emotive Behavior Therapy technique is successful in a school setting. Many of my structured activities are Rational Emotive Behaviorally designed. In July 2004, I received my REBT certificate in education at The Albert Ellis Institute. I had the opportunity to sit in front of the world known Dr. Albert Ellis with a few other graduate, master, and doctorate level students. It was an amazing training with some-one whom we all studied and read about in our higher educational textbooks. To sit, listen, and be trained by a world famous psychological scientist who has proven irrational behavior can be changed was mesmerizing. Not only can irrational behavior be changed individually, but strongly recommended through group work as well.

I have found that we can change behavior, and students have changed when we as professional counselors give the effort to use a paradigm. We can help change behavior when it is interrupted by outside demands changing their natural biological mental mechanisms. By applying positive thoughts we can change irrational students to think rationally and to help them understand their world in a more optimistic view.

Discovering the word "Should" and how it can impact students' behavior

When Dr. Albert Ellis first presented his theory (REBT) in the 1950's he observed the word *should can* have a major negative impact on the human biological thought system. We have found that the word *should* can hold a destructive thought that can make you think irrational. An irrational belief and a demand is a response that can distort reality, prevent you from reaching your goals, develop an unhealthy emotion, and can lead to self-defeating behavior. We find ourselves to get upset because bad things *should* not happen, we just simply get upset and irrational with others because we believe they *shouldn't* happen and it's awful when it does happen. As a counselor working with hundreds of students, and when you add 17 years of my profession, I have worked with thousands of students, and with that, I have found students are facing irrational demands in their neighborhoods. These demands are creating an unhealthy society.

Let's view a case scenario of learned behavior turning irrational:

Today city neighborhoods and some rural communities are so bad it has become a territory ghetto. Today city students are dealing with so many different pressures to fit into society. One of the major fears I have encountered with students is, if they do not wear their pants below their buttocks, or have them sagging, they will face gang related issues or major bullying, antagonizing, and teasing. The sagging pants syndrome came from prison, when inmates were to take their belts off for safety reasons as they entered into their cellblocks. It is almost like students, friends, and youngsters who are under peer pressure *should* be doing what the social environmental change and demands are doing. This becomes a conditioned unhealthy thought process. For these reasons, teenagers are suffering major peer pressure in their communities and neighborhoods. Young teenagers are forced to feel they *must* be doing what the neighborhood is exposing them to. Millions of students are faced with single parents. Most single parent homes create no role model for their kids to feel motivated or inspired to reach their highest goals or potential. Many teenage students who have no curfew and are forced to roam the streets and then try to be accepted by other social groups by engaging into drugs, and crime. Let's think about it for a moment? Unconsciously, the word *should,* appear in our everyday language, and teenagers are feeling they *should* look for other options since they do not have a healthy home life. The *"should"* thoughts are very powerful and demanding. In fact, scientifically proven by Ellis, it can then frustrate anyone if that demand or *should* is not met to fulfill their needs. I like to say, the prison cells are loaded with *"Should"*. In fact, I have counseled students who were involved with street gangs like; The 18 Street Crips, The Bloods, Latin Kings, and many others that demand and control neighborhoods, sell drugs, guns, and bully other teenagers who look vulnerable, or are defenseless.

I came upon and counseled one of many gang related members in New York City. Juan was a skinny Puerto Rican teenager with serious facial acne. His English language was sadly broken and uneducated with major cultural slang. His unwashed oversized jeans were sagging down to his knees, and his Jordan Nike sneakers were some neon colored green with untied laces tucked in on the sides and the shoe tongue sticking out. He was wearing thick heavy gold chains around his neck that weighed in about ten pounds. His walk had a skip after every step. Juan was returning back to school after serving a six month prison term and placed on probation with a mandatory counseling provided by the school principal.

I would ask, explain to me the need of beating up an innocent 15 year old boy walking to school? He answers with an aggressive attitude, "Man, he *should* have been wearing a red shirt and his jeans weren't jacked down when he walks in our hood, we be tight!!" Juan's demand of "should" became an immediate irrational thought. He is automatically conditioned to think about unreasonable situations. Juan becomes bad tempered, building a must and *should* in his biological system. He has been transformed and changed through severe peer pressure. The result, students who are confronted with these *should* demands will be exposed and conditioned to emotional setbacks, societal fear, stress, and academic failure, not to mention, a prison term and other bad behaviors for the kids who are involved with gangs.

Changing Student Lives with A Comprehensive School Counseling Program

I have discovered most inner city schools today do not have a comprehensive school-counseling program. Counselors are running all over the place chasing students down for program or schedule changes, attendance issues or transcript reviews. At times, the counselors look like keystone cops, looking confused, or not knowing where they are going. Schools are not using any theory or groups at all. Schools today need to care about getting the paperwork in order, graduation rates, programming and other important data needed for districts. But, many administrators are blind to the fact and do not know what the students are going through personally. Many supervisors are using uneducated personnel to help guide students who are in need of professional help. Administrators are using working Para's, hallway monitors, secretaries, and attendance teachers all to help children who are suffering with peer pressure, social issues, family issues, and bullying. Basically, mental health counselors are needed, and budgets constrain the hiring.

Not having a comprehensive counseling program in place is a serious problem; the students are in need of professional help, not some "Joe Shmoe" who is standing in the hallway monitoring and disciplining students to get to class on time. In many city schools you might see some male hallway monitor telling students to take their hat off, cursing at them, and talking street slang, actually, it is embarrassing as a professional counselor to see this. Not surprisingly, these uneducated employees are wearing a hat on backwards themselves, expressing sagging pants, cell phone in their hands and cursing like if it were their everyday language.

Counselors are working under pressure from administrators who are requiring them to wear many hats. Counselors are not having much time to help the students who are starving to get psychological relief. I have sat in hundreds of pupil personnel meetings assessing and collaborating on student behavior. It might be important for the social worker, administrator, counselor, and teachers to talk about group counseling. The staff meetings have no strategy for the students to be successful or help in changing their behavior. I truly cry at times with tears to see no extra counselors and no group counseling being performed. Sadly, I might even find some attendance teacher telling me how to handle a certain situation with students. I pause and professionally redirect any uneducated staff on how to handle a student behavioral issue. When I offer and consult other counselors to engage in more group counseling, they seem not to want any worry of group preparations since they have deadlines to catch up on from their supervisor instructions. Today the counselors are so trained to just get their paperwork done.

Many inner city schools have lost the school spirit. Some major high schools are busted up and turned into some type of multi-school system. The students are failing and dropping out because of the lack of resources to help them move forward.

Group counseling is powerful, students are always asking for group time, but the city or other states just do not know how to use it or incorporate it!! Administrators are demanding teachers to counsel an advisory class, but teachers are just not trained or qualified to work advisory. They don't have the lessons, amazing group activities or the education in psychological understanding of student behavior. They are not trained to know the emotional status of student struggles; they don't have the student portfolios, or have been involved with any pupil personnel meetings for the support of the student needs or what might be triggering irrational behavior with certain students. You need professional school counselors to lead group work and incorporate activities that will help have students succeed. I cannot tell you how many teachers have been frustrated emotionally, asking me for help with group activities that can have students respond productively.

Benefits of REBT in group settings

Many educational professionals who are not familiar with Rational Emotive Behavior Therapy, I would like to give you a short description of this technique that can change student lives. Why are students behaving irrational?

The scientific structure of REBT is as follows:

A- *Activating your behavior*. (What has triggered your behavior)

B- *Belief*. (What you think or feel how it is)

C- *Consequences* of the individual's belief. (The result of behavior, upset, irrational etc.)

D- *Disputing* the individual's irrational beliefs. (Challenging the irrational behavior)

E- Stands for the new *effective emotions*. (Changing the irrational belief)

In using the Rational Emotive Behavioral Theory method I have configured the best successful group activities helping students. The REBT in-group activities are certainly constructive, helpful, and successful.

Remember, humans have a biological system to think irrational and our impulse (id) is automatic until we educate ourselves and our ego has developed rationally (Sigmund Freud, 1923). Engaging students in group activities and having them think to choose rationally through positive activities can improve the quality of life.

The purpose of this book and the amazing group activities is to motivate, stimulate and get results in-group counseling that work for students who are struggling in society. I have structured and modified these top 35 group activities that have given me proven results in student success. Students love group activities. Students are always asking for group sessions. I observed that students are very open, and will continue to open up their feelings and emotions through small group work. After specializing in REBT in education, I found creating the group activities around an ABC method is intriguing and positive. The ABC method has developed students to learn why their behavior might have been irrational, and what they can do to help themselves think rationally.

PART 1

THE KINDS OF PROBLEMS SCHOOL CHILDREN HAVE: ENVIRONMENTAL IMPACT ON STUDENTS' DEVELOPMENT

CHAPTER 1

Going to School:
Exposed to Poverty

Let's imagine what most inner city kids go through every morning before going to school.

IT IS 8:00AM Monday morning and many of the inner city school buildings are empty. Attendance at most inner city schools is truant. Most schools are starting to have many counselors calling the students home. Most typical mornings for an inner city student are dreadful. They might hear the sounds of the local trains screaming above on the steel tracks, and feel the vibration of the trains above rattling on the sidewalk. Cars are speeding through the neighborhoods, some passing stop signs or racing and screeching their car wheels, burning rubber down quiet streets beeping their horns to rush someone in front of them. Mobs of 9 to 5 working people are waiting in the middle of the streets to get on crowded buses, and students are walking slowly like zombies with their book bags strapped to their back. Some male students cannot stretch their legs because their pants are sagging below their buttocks. The regular truancy students are hanging out in front of the bodega stores smoking, talking about recent fights, and telling dark stories in street slag, cursing, and spitting on the old cracked concrete pavement. You occasionally hear the sounds of trouble when the red, white and blue police sirens are swirling as they speed by passing red lights. You might hear two guys yelling and screaming at one another in the middle of the streets, or two girls in an early morning catfight pulling each other's hair extensions. You see the retired or welfare residents looking outside their windows enjoying and watching trouble neighborhoods fall apart. The friendly and dirty fat alley cats spying around the neighborhood projects and abandoned lots filled with mixed garbage looking for disease carrying field mice to play and eventually eat. Local residents are walking smoking cigarettes and wearing their nightly stained pajamas still waiting to get washed after wearing them for several weeks. Obese middle-aged minority women and men living on benefit checks walk their aggressive chain linked pit-bull or two, challenging others who might show off their foul foaming mouthy dog. On most streets you might have to walk around dog poop that was never scooped up. Early morning rats the size of raccoons sniff around over loaded garbage cans, and the smell of rotten tomatoes and discarded meat is so awful, you have to squeeze your nose to cut the dreadful odor. At times it can be so smelly; I might have at one point walking to work felt dizzy. In my assessment, and study, I have gathered that when you have concentrations of human garbage, you are just setting yourself up with human diseases. Chronic exposure to poverty causes the brain to lose brain cells and ultimately capture physical change in a detrimental manner. (Singh and Singh 2005, 2006). In one way or another, urban, rural and suburban students are faced with this every day. In fact, with all the diseases, our bodies are only able to fight off some. Students are in danger of unhealthy circumstances, especially when the weather is starting to heat up, students were complaining that when they sleep at night the stink heat was coming off the hefty garbage bags piled from the building super, who continues to fight off rodents running about the piles of tin cans eating the leftovers of spam.

Frustrated teachers are waiting in their empty classrooms to teach kids who come in laughing and smelling of smoke after getting high from an early morning marijuana cigarette. Students who on time sit and finish eating their breakfast as food oozes off their fingers, not prepared, displaying their attitudes with unfilled backpacks never opened since the day before. Some inner city schools and neighborhoods are so violent, kids are afraid to go to school. Students who are considered long-term absence (LTA) are joining different gangs so they don't get bullied or beat up. Single parents, who are struggling to make ends meet, are concerned about themselves and how they are going to have money and food for the next day. Many inner city parents have no education, have several children, and look forward to collect a healthy tax check, food stamps, and welfare funds.

I think we can imagine what these kids are going through at home. That's why I came up with the top 35 amazing group activities that students can relate to. Facts indicate these activities are proven success-helping students get on track to graduation.

Poverty is having an impact on students, and it is important to acknowledge that counselors in our public schools or even some catholic schools are trained to work under a comprehensive school counseling program driven by student data and based on holding counselors to high standards in academic, career, and personal/social development. According to research (Olson, 2000) 22% of students are experiencing stressful life circumstances which are impacting them emotionally, academically, and socially. Most common stressful conditions for students are peer pressure, family issues, academic failures, and social rejections. I truly believe that counselors must keep the door of communication open with their student's parents. Communication is the key too not only understanding your students, but it can also allow you to really hear what your students' parents are saying. If you are strapped with a bilingual situation, team with other staff to communicate. I have gathered and discovered statistically that group counseling is essential for students who are struggling with life challenges as well, whether it is family related or the pressures of dealing with neighborhoods that are toxic and contaminated with hoodlums, drugs and criminal mischief every second of the day. Group counseling sets the stage for better communication, it creates the relationship with other neighborhood teenagers who are going through the same issues, and coming up with solutions.

Counselors are immediately facing challenges as soon as they enter school buildings. In most inner city schools, the day begins for school counselors observing students walking through the metal detectors, security guards with guns, metal scanners, and a common 8:00 am fight between boys or girls in the hallways. In many inner city schools you might find graffiti or murals being drawing on the school walls, empty trophy cases, incomplete outdated bulletin boards, food waste from the lunch room squished on the floor and outdated student work displayed on the hallway walls. In some schools as the class period ends, you might hear music from cell phones in the hallways, or listen to music chosen from the staff from the loud speaker as students change classes from one room to another. It literally creates a street life atmosphere.

A shout out from a male student who just finished taking off his metal buckle belt after being scanned through a metal detector and is most likely a truant: "Hey mister, can you change my program!" These students are always trying to escape the truancy list from classes, or trying to escape failing a class before the marking period ends. Students, who do not want to attend class, are waiting in front of your office with their backpacks filled with school supplies that were never used. After school, counselors battle their way through the multitude of problems that many inner city schools deal with, and mostly with students who are under the chronic stress of everyday life.

These small group counseling interventions focus on increased understanding of student life situations. Students who are struggling with their personal, academic or career goals does not mean they cannot build confidence to contribute in today's society. Since the brain is designed to adapt from experience, it can also change for the better. The secret to student success is being able to manage one's thoughts, feelings, and behaviors.

Incorporating a Rational Emotive Behavior Therapy technique in *some* of the group activities (REBT; Ellis & MacLaren, 1998) is straightforward. The REBT theory helps students who might be facing special educational needs as well. They will learn how some of their learning disabilities affect learning behaviors and classroom performance. It offers a rationale for increasing student awareness and the value of practicing school success skills. REBT emphasizes behavioral change and self-regulation along with the examination and possible modification of thoughts, beliefs, feelings, and expectations.

Scientific Based Research

IN 1978, WHEN Robert Sapolsky the genius award winner of the MacArthur Foundation, a neuroendocrinologist, professor of biology, neuroscience, and neurosurgery at Stanford University, studied baboons in east Kenya Africa. He proved scientifically that stress is extremely dangerous to human health. When we think scientifically of the human body, we think of emotional health is strongly linked to physical health, all because of the psychological component of constant feelings. Today, students suffer this correlation. I wanted to explain the biological system in humans. Robert Sapolsky's theory is outstanding and amazing. I have gathered and compared his theory of stress is scientific evidence that students or kids who are suffering from anxiety, depression, or mood disorders have reasons behind these conditions. I have gathered Sapolsky's evidence of stress and used it to my advantage of explaining the hierarchy system and young students suffering in society. We can understand psychologically what is happening inside the students mind. How they are conditioned and designed to fail. This research by Sapolsky is extraordinary.

A Scientific Primate View:

LET'S RELATE DR. Sapolsky's primate case study to us humans. We have to agree that we are primates, but just a different species.

Sapolsky's baboon study showed how after a few weeks when newborns from different families encounter each other for the first time, they are so excited to see each other. In fact they could barely get around and walk. But something was wrong? One of the families' newborn was from a higher-ranking baboon. This newborn had all the privileges and opportunities as opposed to some others. They eat solid food first, they were able to visit other natural social group areas, and were able to have far more interactions with other baboons. After all, our inner ape, we are born social beings. The baby from the lower ranking baboon was wobbling around socially trying to interact. The baby baboon casually walks over to the higher-ranking infant baboon to play. Conditionally, the mother grabs her daughter and drags her back away from the higher-ranking baby baboon. The poor infant kid has no idea what's happened, but she's just gotten her first lesson in the social hierarchy society. The lower ranking kid is learning, adapting and conditioning herself that she is not somebody who can play with the higher-ranking baboons. The tragedy of such interactions will always be their lasting legacy. According to Sapolsky, years later this can have a major effect and impact on the kids. During the study, when they meet later, scientifically the baboons have conditioned their behavior to not socialize. Eventually, years later when Sapolsky returned back to east Kenya Africa he discovered the lower ranking baboon who is now older, would just stare at the ground, isolating herself from others. The baby baboons mother has accomplished what she was set out for, having her kids stay away from the higher ranking kids. That's what her mom was trying to teach her baby. The mother has taught her baby how to live with low ranking families, poverty and just cope with being low and living that way forever. The baby baboon that is ranked lower in the hierarchy system has become submissive and will develop stress, and eventually get depressed, lonely, develop anxiety, and at times, just be plain ole miserable.

SCIENTIFIC LAB RESEARCH

I just gave you a quick tour of some of the conditioning and change of the evolution in primate study and what can go wrong from a primate's state of mind in the hierarchy system. The literature is built on experiments like this one: Most of the psychologists have read and studied rats during their research days. Scientists use rats for the study of human behavior. Jane Goodall a primatologist played a major factor by eliminating the chimp-study from laboratory study.

Let's take a lab rat in a cage, and from time to time, you give the rat a shock. Nothing major, but nonetheless, the rat's blood pressure goes up and so do stress hormone levels. Evidence tells us, the rat will have the risk of an ulcer. You are giving this rat a stress-related disease because of the sudden shock.

Now, let's take another rat in the second cage. Every time the first rat gets a shock, so does the second rat. Same moderation, same time, both of their bodies are being thrown out of homeostatic balance to exactly the same extent. Both rats are getting sudden shocks when tested.

But there is a serious difference, evidence tells us, every time the second rat gets a shock, it will go over to the other side of the cage, where there's another rat that it can fight and seriously rip the crap out of. Evidence tells us, this rat is not going to get and ulcer or develop any kind of stress. He has an interest or some sort of relaxation to relieve his stress by aggressively going over to someone else and fights to kill.

Using these scientific evidence base experiments, it tells us exactly what the students are facing in society. In short, you are more likely to get a stress response, and more likely to fail.

The first rat has developed some psychological disorders. The first rat has developed isolation, depression, loneliness, anxiety, and other psychological disturbances if you have no outlet, or a shoulder to cry on.

The second rat had an outlet, his symptoms are aggressive, and he will have less of a reaction in stress or none at all. The rat was violent. If there is no control, no predictability, he or she is assessing things are going to get worse. People who are submissive, especially kids, are just sitting there, thinking, here comes trouble, here come the gangs, here comes the ass whipping. I am not going to school, I am afraid. I am staying home. It is automatic failure psychologically, socially, and academically.

So as we view this research, it tells us through rat study, violent students are acting out because of the shock they are going through. The difficulties from society are developing destructive behavior. They will fight off challenges, and protect themselves from stresses or problems.

As we view the scientific study on the first rat, in comparison, humans can develop anxiety and worries, and find themselves isolated. The brain chemistry is altered sheltering them from society.

CHAPTER **3**

The Reason Behind Student Struggles: An Actual Review

THIS IS A critical point of this book: When we take Sapolskys' study on stress and relate it to our social world, we get the same results. Many students today are failing socially, emotionally, and academically because of their relationships in the human hierarchy system. Students are suffering because of the social environment that is contaminated. We are born as social human beings; we then are connected and develop relationships with different groups or stereotypes, just like the baboons have. We might find that many students are born into more opportunity then others. We now know that people are born into some type of social status, whether it is poor, middle class, or rich during human development. We might find many people are so conditioned to live poorly, indicating poor hygiene, and the fashion they are able to afford. Eventually, they assimilate this style of living. When students are faced with a social development that is forced upon them, it becomes distressing. This can lead people to suicide, major depression, and behavioral issues, all linked to stress and the living hierarchy.

As counselors we are supposed to be experts in observation when working with students. We have to recognize that there has to be some kind of biological effect when students are suffering. Sapolsky explains that when people are more dominant the stress hormones are low, and when people are submissive the stress hormones are higher. Clearly, students who are suffering from loneliness, depression, and anxiety seem to be passive, creating higher stress hormonal interaction leading to anxiety, poor social interactions ultimately generating poor mental conditioning and physical health. These students are a perfect example for group sessions. We have to realize when a young adolescent is trapped in an environment of poverty; he or she is facing a huge component of stress as in the lack of control and predictability. In 2003, Sapolsky insists that given the public health consequences, it's time to take this problem seriously. Adding the scientific fact discussed in school group counseling; evidence based results show that students will succeed if enrolled in your group counseling sessions. In group counseling, students explore intellectually and start to think rationally to help relieve their anxiety, understand their social status, depression and feelings of discomfort. Therapy in groups is one good way of relieving stress.

Looking beyond, and reviewing an educational study according to (Bauer, Sapp, & Johnson, 2000) students can and will benefit from group counseling. The studies show that there is a significant amount of change in academics, behavior, and attitude creating a better self, and a high achieving personality. Students are finding their way into the upper status hierarchy system interacting with students who are in a better living condition.

PART 2

THE ROLE OF A SCHOOL COUNSELOR
DURING GROUP ACTIVITIES

CHAPTER 1

The meaning of Group Counseling?

WE DISCUSSED THE Evolution of student behavior; the hierarchy system, a brief description on the biological and the scientific results why students are struggling, and the benefits of group activities. For some leaders in the American School Counseling Association, they have recognized that group counseling involves a number of students working on shared tasks and developing supportive relationships in a group set-

ting. Group counseling is an efficient, effective and positive way of providing direct service to students with academic, career and social/emotional, developmental, and situational concerns.

Group counseling will allow individuals to develop and open up. They will talk about their feelings and share with others. Group counseling is a support system for each other. Group work makes it possible for students to achieve healthier personal adjustments. No matter what kind of morning they had at home, or day issue they are experiencing, just sitting in a circle gives a clear structure and expectation just puts them at ease. In order to get any student to learn, they have to feel safe, and they have to feel respected. Without a safe and respected environment you will not accomplish much academically or help students adapt in society. Remember, without a social emotional growth, there will be no academic growth.

Positive Behaviors

The American School Counseling Association considers group counseling as a primary role for school counselors. According to ASCA, school counselors are models and advocates for student success. Every state in the United States needs to mandate professional school counseling.

I would provide a copy of excellent counseling forms for you to modify to your school policy requirements. The counseling forms will prepare you for your administrator to understand any group counseling that is being performed during your school day. In addition, administrators will be aware of your session, or if they are observing your office, they understand why you are having group sessions in your office.

The Institute of Education at London University gives us confirmation that group counseling does work for students academically, emotionally, and socially. In fact, London University studies show group counseling is more effective than individual counseling (Casey and Berman, 1985).

In order for school counselors to be successful, it is important for counselors to add group work in their daily lesson plans. You might find many school counselors talking or listening to students individually. However, more emphasis is recommended to work with the student's in-group. Individual work is more concentrated for the social worker.

School counselors have a full day of work, especially when programming students, gathering data for special educational students, collaborating with teachers and administrators, record keeping, parents, behavioral issues, completing graduation paperwork, and so much more. However, it is important to find time in their day to incorporate group-counseling work to help develop better social, emotional and academic skills.

At times you might be faced with new administrators who have no idea about counseling, and find your office is filled with 8-10 students. Counseling is just not about paperwork, and filing, it's about helping students succeed in their family, academics, and peers. The administrators need to understand group work helps students get along with others. It might be important to have a sign posted on your doorknob, or door itself, showing that group counseling is in session. This is important for administrators to see, as well as the students.

Learning in Small Groups

I ALWAYS STRUCTURED my weekly Fridays' to be "Group day" with the students. When students are selected for group work, a group of 6 to 10 students is a perfect size that can make group sessions more manageable. The reasonable size of students in group counseling would have the students engage in a more free flow of ideas as opposed to larger groups. Slowly, it can bring more adequate time for students to express themselves. It is important to understand that smaller groups can bring more cohesiveness to each student. Students are more productive in small groups, and learning new behaviors and skills through group counseling proves successful in an ever-changing world. There is more insight, confirming, and corrective messages as opposed to individual counseling.

Types of Counseling

Most school counselors need to try and offer several different types of group counseling activities. Social skills, learning skills, self-control, anger issues, parents, and loss are key parts to any individual who needs counseling or advise to survive in today's tough brutal fast changing society.

It is important to recognize that (Wang, Haertel, and Walberg, 1994), focused on what helps students learn. They found cognition, learning, and social skills to be the most associated with school success. In my activities I built, modified and structured the reasoning rationale, accomplishments, learning, and the societal characteristics of student success.

GROUP DEVELOPMENT

As a counselor you have to paint a picture and become an artist to help students psychologically improve their life. Group settings for students are fascinating and they are intrigued by the activities or gathering of other peers. As a counselor it is important to understand and prepare to lead a group of students to be part of a resolution. Like a teacher or instructor, a lesson plan will create a better-structured group. The activities in this book are successful counseling lesson plans prepared for you to help your group sessions. These plans are always a lesson to have on file for administrators to acknowledge. Your planning will determine how successful your groups will be for the students or clients. Once you have established a group setting, you will find I have gathered my stages of group development to be an excellent set up.

I find these stages are crucial to my success in group counseling. There are three (3) stages of group development. Trust, Work, and Closure are the three key ingredients for successful group interaction. Below you will find a brief guide of the three stages of development for a group setting.

How does group counseling help students?

- I will get students to open up and express their feelings
- Group Counseling recognizes the feelings students are experiencing
- Achieve insight and understanding through others in the group
- When activities are evolving and developing, it releases tension
- It is proven that group activities make you aware of conflicts
- Helps make you conscious of choices and decisions
- Helps you set goals to be successful
- Helps you implement changes

Stages of Group Counseling

Stage 1: Trust-Getting to know you

It is important to have the students to get to know other students in a group. You can set up name tags, this stage will establish a getting to know you. Example: Icebreakers, start with having students pronounce their name and what they like most about themselves or just life in general. Do the same with each student as you go around clock-wise? This creates a warm feeling and comfort emotion for the students to listen to other students briefly. My success is when groups just evolve; this eventually has students inviting themselves back to other sessions or the group that was evolving. I find the students to come back with open arms or wanting more of a group session. As a leader, having the students know each other's name, it creates more trust. The trust stage helps identify goals, and understand one another. (Hint: Focus on the quiet students, as well as the talkative student.)

Stage 2: Work- Productivity

When engaging into the group you will eventually find behavioral changes within the students. You will find students agreeing instead of disagreeing with certain situations during the group activities. You will find students who are quiet open up during certain activities. Group activities will have students who are closed and eventually open up to discussion. When you have developed trust, empathy, and hope, students will gain from feedback, and increase self-awareness and self-disclosure. This stage is crucial in getting students to start their journey into a healthy imagination.

Stage 3: closure- strengthened

The final stage is most important because you would have needed to create a community, sharing and caring. As the leader you would have to summarize or discuss any changes. Once group sessions get going in the right direction the students indicate they want more. After group sessions, they might say, Can we do it again? When can we continue? In fact, I find some students who find themselves in-group sessions get very angry that sessions will no longer continue. However, you can continue the topic for the following session, and closure in some groups could last longer than one group session.

CHECKLIST

Once you have gathered your students, analyzed profiles, group session forms are in place, documents, teacher and administrator referrals are collected, records, and transcripts you are now ready to set the stage for students to enter group sessions. Review the sample forms I have provided: I found these forms to be an excellent way to incorporate and establish some form of foundation to a comprehensive school counseling program. The parent permission form, evaluation form, and the counseling program form. These forms will best serve you for filed documentation. These forms can be modified to your school standards. After the students have completed their group counseling applications and getting approved, and signed signatures by their parents, you will then need to keep each students application on file for information required if there should be any modifications, adjustments, or amendments. For example, you might come across an administrator who might want to know if the student and their parents have agreed to certain group sessions that might involve more open discussion. Another example would be additional information needed if there should be a conference with a school psychologist or special educational evaluation plan (IEP)

RULES

The students need to understand and respect the group rules. For example, listening to each other and no negative put downs on each other. Everything discussed in the group stays within the group. There is only positive communication to help one another.

I have accumulated some helpful discussion questions for icebreakers that students seem to respond to:

1. What can we do to help each other get the most from this group?
2. What do you think can happen if we have negative statements towards one another?
3. How can we develop trust in our group?

Refreshments

I always like to have refreshments for the students. Students love refreshments like pretzels and bottled water. Refreshments make the kids start to feel warm and comfortable with one another. In fact, it starts a social gathering before any group session gets under way. It is important that every student remain in the circle. The circle is like a magnet; it truly pulls in the students to open up why things in their life might not be right or setting them off to the wrong path. The circle creates the student to express their feelings and ideas, and they learn how to listen to one another. The students will feel more in control of their thoughts and behaviors. I have gathered that group sessions last about one-classroom period. (45/48 minutes). Some instructors or counselors go only 20/30 minutes, but the students are only just getting started in 20/30 minutes. The circle cannot be broken; otherwise you will not be able to have icebreakers, shared communication, or develop trust between others. The students need to understand that the circle cannot be broken. At times you might find students to not completely sit in a circle. You find some students to get up. They might leave the group without asking. Group work is a powerful tool to keep students under control emotionally.

Your group session needs to consist of no more than 8 students; data has given us the smaller the group, the better results. Larger groups seem to get out of control, and you will find lesser results in student success. Begin by introducing yourself, and welcoming the students, explaining what the goals are for the group sessions. Icebreakers are very important in-group counseling. The warm up will get the students comfortable in a circle setting. The students seem to like the idea of introducing themselves. Kids love to talk about themselves. You might have gathered some students from other areas or classrooms where they do not interact with other students. So, getting the students to introduce themselves would most certainly make them comfortable.

You can open up your session with many ideas. You have to try and make it interesting. Think about your warm-up for the students: Self-concept, conflict resolution, sexual harassment, student success, race issues, cultural issues, and family issues. (Review my best Icebreakers, Kids love them.)

PART 3

ICE BREAKERS, THEMES, AND ACTIVITIES

Icebreakers

ICEBREAKERS PLAY AN important role during a group counseling session. Icebreakers get the students comfortable in their new surrounding environment. They start to listen, communicate, and feel relaxed so they can open up. At times you might find during an icebreaker a student really opens up, be sure to continue with that student as group continues. During your group counseling session, you might want to think about a timeline. An icebreaker can only last up to 20-25 minutes (Try to make them shorter), if you have a larger lesson planned, then your icebreakers should be no longer than 10 minutes. From there you can start your prepared activity. Review some of the icebreakers that are very successful.

Spider Webs

In this icebreaker, you need to have a spool of yarn, string, or wool. Ask the students to stand in a circle or if possible, students can be seated. Hold on to the end of the string and throw the spool to one of the students to catch. They then choose a question provided for them on a large post it chart paper from 1-10 to answer. A list of 10 sample questions is given below. You can modify the questions for your group population or situations. Holding the end of the string, after each question is answered, students then continue to toss the yarn to one another in the group. Eventually this creates a web. At the end of the game you could comment that we all played a part in creating this unique web and if one person were gone it would look different.

Some helpful questions that can get Spider webs going:

1. If you had a time machine, what point in the future or in history would you visit?

2. If you had a chance to go anywhere in the world, where would you go?

3. If your home were burning down, what three objects would you try and save?

4. If you could talk to any one person that might be important to you who would it be and why?

5. If you had to give up one of your 5 senses (hearing, seeing, feeling, smelling, tasting) which would it be and why?

6. If you were an animal, what would you be and why?

7. Do you have a pet? If not, what sort of pet would you like?

8. Can you name a gift that will stay with you forever?

9. Name one thing you really like about yourself?

10. What's your favorite thing to do in the summer?

Flags/United Nations

Flags are a get-to-know-you activity, helping students express what's important to them or more about themselves.

I find this activity is important because of the many cultures, religion, and diversity in today's society.

Procedure

1. Provide large sheets of paper, crayons, markers, and paints.

2. Ask each student to draw a flag of their origin, which contains some symbols or pictures describing who they are, what's important to them or what they enjoy?

3. Each flag is divided into 4 or 6 segments. Each segment can contain a picture of favorite emotions or favorite food.

4. It can also include a hobby, a skill, where you were born, your family, and your faith. Give everyone 20 minutes to draw his or her flag.

5. Ask some of the group to share their flags and explain the meaning of what they drew.

6. It is always nice to have students get up and pin their drawing and discuss in presentation form. (Note: If a student refuses to present, do not force him or her to do so)

Word Chain links

This is a word association game. Your group should already be sitting in a circle. The first person starts with any word they wish, For example: Black. The next person repeats the first word and adds another word which links to the first word. For example: Board. The next person repeats the previous word and adds another word, For example: Crayon, and so on. Remember, everything needs to be linked. Try to move quickly, only allow five seconds for each word link.

Grab Bag Stories

Try to always have a bunch of objects or toys so you can play grab bag and tell a story when group evolves in your office setting. Try to always have your bag available in your office. My office was always filled with games and toys. This icebreaker goes well with one of the 35 amazing group activities. Your collected objects and toys need to be placed in a one of your favorite old bags. The objects can include everyday items, for example, a pen, a doll, a pinecone, mobile phone, a fossil, holiday light, and Halloween mask! Pass the bag around the group clockwise and invite each student to dip their hand into the bag (without looking inside) and pull out one of the objects you have collected. The leader begins a story, which includes his object. After 15-20 seconds, the next student takes up the story and adds another 15-20 seconds, incorporating the object they are holding. Everyone has made a contribution to your epic literary tale. This is a great icebreaker!! And this can lead into a complete group activity.

Who am I?

1. This icebreaker will go great with another amazing group activity "something positive". For this activity, you will need crayons, paints, and markers, colored pens, scissors and white index cards (5x8.)

2. Give each young person an index card. Ask them to draw and cut out a life-sized shape of a face. They can also cut out eyes and a mouth if they wish, or if they feel very creative.

3. Each student is then asked to decorate his or her cut out face. One side (Outside) of the face represents what they might think people see/know/believe about them. The other side of the face represents how they feel about themselves? For example, what feelings are going on inside of them? What people do not necessarily know or see?

4. This is best used in an established group where the students are comfortable and at ease with each other.

Pass the Apple

This icebreaker is popular but it still remains to make the students comfortable, and I have found success using this icebreaker. Ask the students to form a circle. Give the students a large apple or grapefruit and explain they need to pass this around the circle. Hint: For junior/ seniors. No problem!! BUT, it has to be passed around the circle using only chin and neck. If the apple or grapefruit is dropped, it must be returned to the previous player in the circle and the game restarts. This icebreaker creates cohesiveness, communication, strategy, and developing friendship.

PART 4

35
AMAZING
GROUP
ACTIVITIES

1. SOMETHING POSITIVE

OBJECTIVE: Students will recognize positive attributes about their classmates.

MATERIALS: White sheet of paper/ paper plates, colored markers, and tape

CLASSROOM SET-UP: This group activity should be worked with 8 students/advanced counselors or teachers can use a full class roster.

PROCEDURE:

1. Have students sit at their desks or in a group. Hand out a white sheet of paper. Ask the students to draw an image or special object that would represent them in a positive way.

2. Instruct students to draw on their white sheet of paper. If you have advanced art supplies ready for use, have the students be creative to use the material provided

3. The object or image should symbolize a specific quality in them. It would be best if the students can share with the group, and present their drawing.

4. The counselor, social worker, or teacher explains to the students that their images or drawing can be for the classroom decorations as well as your office.

5. Show sample positive drawing: I usually draw a large oak tree for the students to get an idea; an oak tree symbolizes me as

someone who is strong and healthy. This is a positive image. (You might have a different positive drawing.) Explain to the students that all drawings and images are to be positive, no negative drawings or images are accepted. This creates and conditions students to only think positive about them and not negative. Once again this is an amazing reconditioning activity!!

6. Have the students tape their images or drawing to the wall as they present and leave all drawings for your decorations. If the students want their drawings back, let them keep it for their own positive re-enforcement

MAIN ACTIVITY

1. The 8 students should be divided into two groups. If there are an odd number of students, join in.

2. Have one group of students form an inner circle. Then have the other group form an outer circle around the inner circle. (Each student needs to be behind one another).

3. Each student should have a colored marker (Black), and a white sheet of paper or paper plates with tape to their back.

4. Tell the students to write at least one positive word on the paper/ plates taped to those students back in front of them. For example: Ask the students to write something positive about that person in front of you?

5. Emphasize to the students that there should be no negative words written allowed. (If there are negative words, counselors and teachers should end the group session or disqualify that certain student)

6. Explain to the students that they would need to shift or rotate their circle to the next student in front of them.

7. If you want to participate, follow the same procedure as the students

8. Closely monitor the writing of the students to be sure they are writing positive words

9. Continue the activity until the outer circle has finished and the inner circle has stepped back and completed their positive words.

10. At the end, have the students take their papers/plates off their backs, sit back in a circle and silently read what their classmates have written about them.

KEY QUESTIONS TO ASK:

1. What happened?

2. How do you feel about your sheet/plate?

3. How did you feel about the activity?

4. What happened between people?

5. How can we use what we did in the activity help us?

DISCUSSION QUESTIONS:

1. Which words on your paper/plate surprised you most?

2. Which words would you agree? And why?

3. Who would think wrote the surprising words?

CLOSING:

1. What is your favorite word on the paper?

2. What word surprises you most?

2. HOW I SEE MYSELF

OBJECTIVE: To see and understand ourselves

MATERIALS: If you can provide a small mirror for each student, paper, and pencil

PROCEDURE:

1. If you do not have a small mirror for each student then you may have one and pass it around. Each student should briefly look at them-selves

2. Have each student write down (4) positive things he or she saw when looking in the mirror

3. Once again have each student think again and have each one to identify (4) positive assets about themselves. For example: something you own, good skater, listener, leader, etc.

4. Now ask, write down (4) negative things they didn't like when they looked in the mirror. For example: not good in sports, poor in math, etc.

5. Have the students draw a big circle and mark down several pluses and minuses about themselves inside the circle.

QUESTIONS:

1. Explain what is harder to identify, the positive or negative traits?

2. What does it say about you if you have negative traits?

3. Do you think it is possible for anyone to have all positive traits? All negative traits?

4. Explain what positive traits you are most proud of?

5. Explain what negative trait you would most want to change to a positive?

6. Can you think of a time when you were a negative person?

7. Explain when you have done some positive things in your life, and how it made you feel good.

3. LET'S TALK TO PARENTS

OBJECTIVE: To examine some of the problems we might have with our parents

MATERIALS: chart paper or newsprint/markers

TOPICS:

1. When I am upset with my parent, I.............................
2. When my parent gives me advise I...........................
3. I am afraid to tell my parent anything because.......................
4. I need to talk with my parents about ....
   ...
5. I like to talk to my parent when he or she is ....

PROCEDURE:

1. Have students or counselor pick a topic. Have the students make that decision.

2. Explain to the students that they would need to find a partner to pair up or team with.

3. Each student is to talk to one another for 2 minutes while the other listens actively without interfering or saying anything

4. After the 2 minutes is recorded, the other student will have 2 minutes to speak on the same topic

COMMUNICATING WITH PARENTS CAN BE A VERY DIFFICULT SITUATION:

1. Why do we have difficulty communicating with parents?

2. What did you discover about the way you communicate with your parent?

3. What do you think makes us fearful to speak with our parents about certain things?

4. How can we solve any problems or issues if we don't talk honestly to each other?

5. How can we improve our relationship with our parents?

6. Explain what you might think is the best way to talk with our busy parents?

7. Explain if you needed to change one thing about your parent communicating with you, what would it be?

4. LET'S TALK POSITIVE AND NEGATIVE

OBJECTIVE: To identify positive and negative ways of influencing others behaviors

MATERIAL: Create a handout sheet that fits your student case load problems: Agree or Disagree or Uncertain

PROCEDURE

1. Students will complete handouts
2. In small groups of (3) have students interact on the agree/disagree/uncertain handout sheets
3. Have the whole group discuss and determine which items on the worksheet are the most positive methods of influencing someone else

DISCUSSION QUESTIONS

1. How much control do you think you really have over someone else's behavior?
2. Explain why you think street gangs are influential?
3. What positive means of influencing others exist?
4. How can a name influence you?

PERSONAL QUESTIONS

1. Explain why you would influence others?

2. Thinking about influencing others, explain why you would think a positive or negative of influencing is more successful?

3. Explain a time when you might have influenced someone else's behavior?

5. DO YOU KNOW WHO YOU ARE?

NOTE: Discuss with the students that they are in their primary stages of development. Explain that they eventually will be independent, and have their own ideas. Explain to the students that they have to understand some of their thinking, feeling, and behavior, in order to find out more about themselves.

OBJECTIVE: To learn how to accept oneself

MATERIAL: Provide a lunch bag for each student, cut small slips of paper for students to write on

PROCEDURE:

Outside

1. Give students sets of material (lunch bag)

2. Ask students to think about how they look on the outside of themselves (an image you project to others)

3. Explain to the students that they would need to write words or draw symbols representing these characteristics on the outside of their bags.

INSIDE of the Bag

1. Explain to the students now they can think about who they are on the inside.

2. Have students explain or talk about their feelings, problems, issues, high/low points, or your personality traits that you might keep hidden from others

3. On the small pieces of cut paper, have the students write these issues on the cut slips of paper and place them inside of their bag

OUTSIDE of the bag

1. Have the students share the outside of their bags as much of the content as possible. Some students might feel uncomfortable, so you might want to get others who are more open to the activity

2. The students will display their bags and read the words on the outside of the bag

INSIDE/OUT

1. After the students discuss the contents outside of their bag, they then can discuss the contents inside of the bag or outside; whatever they feel is most important to them. It will just evolve.

QUESTIONS:

1. If someone would perceive you as having basically a negative quality, does that make you a useless individual?

2. Discuss if you consider the descriptions or contents basically positive or negative

3. Explain that it is important for students to understand people are meaningful regardless of their abilities or their actions. People can always change to improve things. But, even if they didn't, they would still be important.

4. Discuss what is meaningful, worthwhile, and important?

5. Have the students discuss what was more difficult to think about placing their feelings outside or inside of the bag?

6. What do you think it is about the things on the inside that people want to protect? As opposed to being open about them?

7. Are there some people who have access to all or some of the things you put inside the bag?

6. THE AUDITION

OBJECTIVE: To develop an understanding of an individual/students decision

MATERIALS: None

PROCEDURE:

1. Group members would act out and analyze to situations created by the group. Explain to the students that they have to audition for an upcoming television series.

2. One of the group members will volunteer to be the director or group leader. He or she will read a script or scene the students make up, and the members would have to respond.

3. The actors of the script or scene will not read from the script or scene. However, they are able to respond to the situation, as they want.

4. The key points should be placed on the response, exploring their kinds of responses, and examining the character responding to the script.

SUGGESTED IDEAS AND QUESTIONS:

1. You expectantly find your friend stealing your watch. What do you do? How would you react?

2. You find a letter that was recently written by your boyfriend telling someone else how he is beginning to like her. What do you do? How would you react?

3. You are at a party and someone hands you a drink/drugs? What do you do? How would you react?

Variations:

1. Write new scenes that may be more appropriate to your group setting

2. Have 2 people in a particular scene

3. Explain to the group they can write out their own scripts

4. Talk to the English department about any scripts they may have to help students get ideas

7. LET'S TALK SELF ESTEEM

OBJECTIVE: Self-esteem, self-image, values, discussing attitudes, feelings, and concerns using the stock market

MATERIALS: Index cards (3x5 or 5x8) write down company names. Wall street journal articles on companies.

PROCEDURE:

1. Break students up into groups
2. Discuss to the group what owning stock shares is all about
3. Discuss the concept of shares, and how owning stock shares really make you part owner of a company
4. Give each group two (2) stock certificates and ask them to reflect upon each company they own. The group would then share and talk about what their company is all about. You can ask if the group wants to trade with other groups.
5. Each member of the group would have to discuss why they personally want to be shareholders of the company
6. Each member would suggest what the company can do to help others

COMPANY STOCK IDEAS:

1. Facebook
2. Twitter
3. Nike
4. Educational industries
5. Potato-chip world

6. Travel

7. Alcohol industries

IDEAS:

1. Group members could create their own company

2. Group members can vote on issues raised at the annual stock-holders meeting

.

8. SELF IMAGE

OBJECTIVE: Values, self-image, first hander, or second hander

MATERIALS: Grade level of choice, short story

PROCEDURE:

1. Instructor would read the following interesting short story of their interest and ask the group to discuss each character. By agreement with the group, they will list in rank order the worst to the best:

2. For example: names of the characters in the short story

3. The groups would discuss who is the best and worst character, and compare their list of best to worst to the other groups best and worst

4. The students would then interact with one another and discuss why the characters values are good? Etc.

5. This interaction would be an ideal situation for other students to unconsciously talk about their own values, and self-image.

9. LET'S MAKE A DECISION

OBJECTIVE: To have students make independent decisions

MATERIALS: Envelopes, or index cards

PROCEDURE:

1. As the group leader, explain to the students that they are lost in some large city. The cities can be New York City, Los Angeles, Chicago, or Philadelphia, etc.

2. The students are then given envelopes or index cards

3. The students must understand that survival is needed in large cities

4. After the items are given to each student, the group leader is to explain why he gave that particular item to that particular student.

ITEMS ON INDEX CARDS:

1. A loaded gun

2. A medical kit

3. A transmitter that needs to get fixed

4. A book how to survive in the city

5. Hammer, nails and wood

6. Navigation system/train matches

7. Flash light/matches

8. Gold

9. Puppy

10. Map

VARIATIONS/CHANGES

1. Create a new list of items found in the envelope

2. Have the groups decide who is to receive each item

10. UNDERSTANDING OUR VALUES

OBJECTIVE: To have students understand their values

MATERIAL: Play money $500 plus, index cards with the values to be sold and written on them such as: Riches, complete stereo system, any talent, fame, brains, president, peace on earth, end to poverty, marijuana, new body, school principal, power, new car, maid service, etc.

PROCEDURE:

1.   Distribute $500 in play money to each group member

2.   Explain to group of students that they can offer to buy or purchase any item written on the index card. If they try to buy it at the end of everyone offering a price, then they must purchase that item

3.   Read to the group each item

4.   They may want to add or omit some items

5.   After all the money is collected, ask the group members to talk about the items they have purchased

6.   Group members may want to trade, however, what is worth more value to them?

VARIATIONS:

1.   Group members may trade the items with each other at the end of the sale

2.   Identify which items can be bought or obtained in real life situations

11. CLARIFYING OUR VALUES AND FEELINGS

OBJECTIVE: To identify various values to relate to similar situations

MATERIALS: Index cards

PROCEDURE:

1. The instructor either reads, describes, or hands out index cards of similar situations

2. Students in groups are first given a situation without knowledge of what the second similar situation would be

3. After discussing the first situation, the second is introduced

4. The group then discusses the difference between the two situations placing emphasis on the different values which are part of each situation

SOME SITUATION IDEAS:

1. Someone breaks into your home and steals money you have been saving for some time. How does this make you feel?

2. Someone has made a false complaint about you, and this has made you get into a great deal of trouble? How would you feel?

3. You admire a classmate's fashion, and you tell him/her so. He/she thanks you and pays you a compliment in return. How do you feel?

IDEAS:

Have some of the students create their own situation and role play

12. ARE YOU AGGRESSIVE, PASSIVE, OR ASSERTIVE?

OBJECTIVE: having students develop skills in communication and handling stressful situations

MATERIALS Index cards:

PROCEDURE:

1. Explain to the students various ways of verbally reacting to stressful situations, aggressively, positively, and assertively.

2. Have students act out all three behaviors.

3. Index cards are labeled: aggressive, passive, and assertive

4. Each group member will react according to the type of card he received.

5. Read a situation and ask each member to react

6. Have the rest of the groups identify the type of reaction each has demonstrated and discuss the feelings associated with each reaction

7. Then collect the index cards and have another group identify, and respond to a new situation

SITUATIONS:

1. Your math grade is lower than what you deserved. How do you approach your teacher? What do you do?

2. Your friend borrows some school supplies, and she never returned the supplies, and you got in trouble because you needed it for class. She wants to borrow the supplies again. How do you deal with her/him?

3. Your parents blame you for not getting a class grade you deserve, because they think you were goofing around in school? How do you deal with that?

IDEAS:

1. Have group members come up with their own ideas or situations, and have them create a behavior
2. Have different members react to the same scene

13. SELF-AWARENESS AND GOALS

OBJECTIVE: To become aware of the process in obtaining a goal

MATERIAL: Index cards

PROCEDURE:

1. Explain to the group that designer names have higher value on their product than other non-designer names on labels

2. A person doesn't wear jeans, he wears Calvin Klein's

3. Famous people design their own products such as: The Kardashians, Gucci, and Nike

4. Break a class up into groups and ask them to select a goal or create their own. Have students create the steps needed to reach their goal

5. Basically have them create their own designer brand/product

   GOALS: LeBron James of becoming an Olympic athlete

STEPS:

1. Think about what you are good at?

2. Practice

3. Join a team or club

4. Latest equipment

5. Eat the right foods

6. Once the steps are formed, ask that each step be written on a separate index card

7. At the end of the activity, have each student present their title and method
8. Have the groups discuss their methods of reaching goals

TOPICS/IDEAS FOR ACTIVITY:

1. Good student   growing up   friends
2. Actor   rich   independent
3. Teacher   anger   happy
4. Job   freedom   parents/etc.

14. LET'S PLAY A GAME

OBJECTIVE: Having students develop listening and communication skills

MATERIAL: Index cards/sheet of writing paper/pens and markers

PROCEDURE:

1. Have each student share their experiences about themselves through an introduction
2. Explain to the students that each game host usually introduces the players of the game, in a few sentences or so.
3. In this case the group members will pair off with someone they are not familiar with.
4. Have each member talk to their partner for 2 or 3 minutes as some sort of interview
5. After, each group member will introduce their partners, after they learned about one another
6. Explain to the students/group that they should try to avoid hobbies, pets, favorite color etc. This can drag the introduction, and take a lot of time

SAMPLE INTRODUCTION CARD:

1. Tell the group about what you like to do in your spare time
2. Share with the group about your background such as: where you live? Who is in your family?
3. Responsibilities/job
4. Likes and dislikes

5. Explain to the group that you would like to collect their cards or profile from each of the member in the group.

6. You then can read to the group as they try to figure out who the person is?

PROFILE SHEET IDEAS

1. My favorite hobby is_____

2. I plan to be a_____

3. My current job position_____

4. My college goals are_____

15. LET'S TALK THE RIGHT WAY

OBJECTIVE: To have students recognize that their irrational statements can lead into hurting people emotionally, socially, and academically

MATERIAL: Index cards

PROCEDURE:

1. Explain to the students/groups how they felt when someone would tell them to "keep quiet" or just yell at them for no good reason

2. Explain to the students/groups if there were other experiences that might have angered them or got them upset when someone might have told them some irrational statements

3. As the group leader, you talk about some irrational words that might hurt someone's feelings. For example: "I don't believe you" how can we re-phrase this statement? One idea might be: "I think you're wrong". Or "you're mistaken" changing the words can make your communication much more professional, and rational.

RE-WORDING-EXERCISE IDEA'S

a. I hate you! / I do not like how you are talking

b. You can't do that /wouldn't it be better if you...

c. I challenge you/ That is not a good idea

OTHER IDEA'S

1. Read a story that will have several irrational words, and have the

group recognize these words and have them interact with one another, and come up with a better rationalized solution

2. Have the group come up with their own words, and have others re-word the irrational statements

16. LOWER YOU'RE TONE

OBJECTIVE: To understand the tone of someone's conversation through volume, and voice

MATERIAL: None

PROCEDURE:

1. Explain to the students/groups how communicating through your tone of voice can steer the conversation

2. Explain to the group that they will have to make a determination what tone of voice is happening and where the conversation can lead into simply by listening to their voice

3. Explain you would like 2 volunteers to leave the room, and then present them with a situation they must act upon.

SITUATION IDEA'S

1. Someone smashed into your bike, you are feeling fine, but angry that your bike is smashed

2. You are with your boyfriend/girlfriend and tell him/her that you like him

3. You are a student and ask lots of questions

4. You are not sure what to do and argue against smoking marijuana or drinking alcohol

MORE IDEA'S

1. Have your group come up with their own idea situations

2. Have index cards with certain situations and scenes

3. Have more students get involved with the scenes

4. This activity can be worked on two or three sessions

17. LET'S HAVE A DEBATE

OBJECTIVE: learning communication skills

MATERIAL: None

PROCEDURE:

1. As the group leader ask two (2) volunteers to enter into a debate while other group members watch and listen
2. Have the debaters select a topic from a list you shall provide, so they can get their thoughts together
3. As the group leader you provide and describe the rules of the debate

RULES:

1. Each debater sits the opposite from one another
2. Each debater states his points without listening to his opponent
3. The group leader will then tell the debaters to switch, then each debater will take the other opponents view points
4. At the end of the debate, group members tell how they felt when they were speaking or noticed the other person was not listening.

TOPICS IDEA'S:

1. New York sport teams are the best vs. New York teams are not the best
2. Parents have the right to go into your room vs. parents have no right going into your room
3. Smoking around people vs. not smoking around people

4. Teenagers should have a curfew vs. teenagers should not have a curfew

5. Liquor should not be sold past 10:00pm vs. liquor can be sold past 10:00pm

6. Minors should drink large gulp soda vs. minors should not drink large gulp soda

7. Driver license should not be given until the age of 21 vs. driver license should be given out at the age of 21

18. ARE WE AGREEING OR NOT?

OBJECTIVE: To develop skills in agreeing with others

MATERIAL: Pen or pencils, or large paper

PROCEDURE:

1. Explain to the group that they get a report card that rates them for the year

2. Explain to the group that they can now create their own report card about the school

3. Explain to the group that they can rate the school by it's: cleanliness, staff, programs, etc.

4. As a group leader get a group member to record any agreements for each category

VARIATIONS:

1. Each group member can develop his own report card

2. Have the group create a variety of topics outside from the school setting

3. Compare and contrast two (2) different groups of report cards

19. DO YOU HAVE GOALS?

OBJECTIVE: To have students identify personal goals

MATERIAL: Index cards

PROCEDURE:

1. Explain to the group that they will take a trip
2. The trip will take several days, and there will be stops on the way
3. Explain to the group that they would anticipate all needs
4. Explain to the group that a large family is on this trip, and that they will eat homemade food along the way, and not stopping at any restaurants
5. Explain to the group that they will have to write on the index cards the items and preparations for the trip

ITEMS:

1. A road map
2. Credit card
3. Money
4. Car
5. Clothes
6. Hotel reservations
7. Vacation time
8. Cooler
9. Utensils
10. Napkins

IDEA'S

1. Explain to the group that they would have to make a decision about some real goals and imaginary goals.

2. Have the group create their own, and interact with one another

◆————————◆

20. BODY IMAGES

OBJECTIVE: To have students focus on their positive attributes as factors that can contribute to developing positive self-esteem

MATERIAL: Pencils/Pen/Paper/Envelopes

PROCEDURE:

1. Have students write down some attributes that are not related to physical appearance

2. Explain to the your group of students that everyone in the group will get an envelope and write their names on the front of the envelope

3. After the students write their names on the front of the envelopes, they will then need to place the envelopes on a table or classroom desk in the middle of the group circle

4. After you provide the material required, you will ask the students to write down one positive thing they like about each member of the group

5. Explain to the group they should think about special talents, interests, qualities, and unique personal characteristics, not on appearance

6. Ask the group members to place their notes in each of their group members envelopes

7. Explain to the group that there should be no negative notes

8. Explain to the group at the end of the activity, group members will get their envelopes back and see what others think of them

9. When the group receives their envelopes they need to write down their own positive self-esteem images and make a list of 5 things they can do to help build positive self-esteem within themselves

IDEA'S:

1. Try to encourage the group of students to keep a journal of their own positive self-esteem, and for them to come in periodically to review with you some of their feel good values they have built for themselves

21. LET'S IDENTIFY YOUR POSITIVE PERSONAL TRAITS

OBJECTIVE: Having students build a geo-gram or shield of positive traits

MATERIAL: A diagram for students to draw and write down some of their positive proud moments, accomplishments, and goals

PROCEDURE:

1. Give each student a diagram with at least six (6) boxes so they can draw and write down some of their positive traits

2. Explain in box 1, they can draw a symbol of a goal of theirs

3. Explain in box 2, they can draw a symbol of something they are proud of

4. Explain in box 3, they can write a word that best describes them

5. Explain in box 4, they can draw a picture or write the name of an animal

6. Explain in box 5, write the names of family members

7. Explain in box 6, they can draw what they like to do

8. After their diagram is complete, they can present, display or describe their positive diagram

OTHER IDEAS

1. The group can create their own categories

2. The group can create new diagrams at home and begin the group on what they did at home

22. ARE WE ALL GROWN UP?

OBJECTIVE: To have students recognize their stage of maturity

MATERIAL: None

PROCEDURE:

1. As the group leader, it is important to discuss the stages of development, and maturity around other people. How do they speak? How do they act?

2. Explain to the group how their age might determine how they act in a certain situation

3. Explain how a child would react to a situation? Scream, yell, go into tantrum

4. Explain how a teenager would react to a certain situation? Get aggressive, yell, scream, punch a wall

5. Explain how an adult might rationalize a bad situation. An adult engages into a rationalized conversation, stay quiet, etc.

6. Explain that age really has nothing to do with grown up, and that it is the behavior of any individual. In fact, many young people react with maturity in certain situations, and adults will act irrational

SITUATIONS:

1. Your mother tells you that you are not old enough

    _____

2. The law says you cannot drink alcoholic beverages

    _____

3. Your teacher tells you that your behavior is inappropriate, please leave the room _____

4. Your parents tell you that you are not of age, and that you will not attend a party that is not chaperoned

VARIATIONS

1. Group members can create their own stories

2. Group members can create their own scenes and have other members react to these scenes

3. Group members can cite other examples of where age and maturity are related, such as voting, military services, running for public office, etc.

23. WHAT IS THE IMPRESSION OF YOUR-SELF?

OBJECTIVE: To identify positive feelings

MATERIAL: Index cards and sentence completions

PROCEDURE:

1. Explain to the group that they will work together and try and put some sentence structures together
2. Explain to the group that you will be giving them some incomplete sentences about themselves
3. Everyone in the group is to complete the incomplete sentence
4. After the sentences are completed the groups will then discuss in details with each other

SENTENCE IDEAS:

1. My favorite time of the day is_____
2. My favorite color is_____
3. My favorite food is_____
4. My favorite TV. Program is_____
5. My favorite subject is_____
6. Someone I trust is_____
7. Someone I love is_____
8. Someone I helped is_____
9. Someone I talked to_____
10. Smoking cigarettes is_____

24. PERSONAL STRENGTHS

OBJECTIVE: Students will learn more about themselves and take a self-assessment questionnaire. Also, students will identify personal strengths and indicators of those strengths

MATERIAL: A copy of a worksheet to each student

PROCEDURE:

1. Explain to the students that they would need to break-up into small groups of four (4) to share their self-assessments

QUESTIONS:

1. Was it difficult to select the five terms that best describe you?

2. How was it for you to think of the indicators?

3. How did you select the terms that least characterizes you?

4. Which question is the biggest asset to you as you move into the next stage of your life?

5. Which question might describe you and indicates that you might want to work on?

6. Which question might describe you and indicates that you might want to work on for the future?

7. Which question might you be proud of? Explain?

25. WHAT IS IN THAT GRAB BAG?

OBJECTIVE: Students will grab an item from a mystery grab bag and discuss what it they have is. This situation can lead into something about them

MATERIAL: A grab bag with item such as: a doll, a box of cigarettes, a coffee cup, a pen a toy truck, etc.

PROCEDURE:

1. Explain to the group that they will pick a mystery item from a grab bag

2. Explain to the students after they pick the mystery item from the grab they will need to talk about that item

3. The item can be a coffee cup? This cup can lead into something about their lives

QUESTIONS:

1. What was the message?

2. How did the group members feel when they picked out their item

3. Did the texture make them grab the item they pulled out

IDEA'S:

1. HAVE STUDENTS GRAB AND ITEM AND PASS THE BAG AROUND

26. LET'S TALK DIFFERENT FAMILIES

OBJECTIVE: Students in a group will learn about other families through the eyes of other group members

MATERIAL: None or (optional) index cards with family type names on them

PROCEDURE:

1. Explain to the students that they should break up into 3 or 4 small groups

2. Explain to the group that you (group leader) will call out to each group the type of family they might have chosen

3. Do not assign specific roles for the students in the group

4. Explain to the students that they would have to work out the type of family they choose, and each member would have to role play

5. Families they choose would have to be: family of ants, family of clowns, family of substance abusers, family of alcoholics, or anything that is bazaar.

6. Explain to the group, once one group role plays their family, the next group will do the same

QUESTIONS:

1. How was the family acting? Explain

2. Was the family cold? Explain

3. Did the family love? Explain

4. Was the family warm? Explain

5. Was the family independent? Explain

6. Was the family angry? Explain

7. How did the other people feel as they were watching other group members discuss their family? Explain

27. LET'S RATIONALIZE A SITUATION

OBJECTIVE: Students will learn a way to get out of certain situations

MATERIAL: Index cards with certain situations

PROCEDURE:

1. Explain to the students they must break into 3 or 5 groups
2. Explain to the students each group will be presented on an index card with certain situations
3. Explain to the students that each group will interact and plan a way to help the situation presented
4. Explain to the groups, after they come up with a plan, the group will choose a leader to present their case

SITUATIONS:

1. People trapped on a high mountain because one member dropped their climbing rope
2. People having an unapproved party and find out their parents are coming home in 10 minutes
3. Students who failed a class and are afraid to go home
4. People who have bad situations at home
5. Something went wrong
6. Who is to blame?
7. That is not fair!!
8. What else can we do?
9. I hate animals
10. Let's go drink with the girls/guys

28. YOUR SCHOOL

OBJECTIVE: Students will learn how behavior affects student achievement and school climate

MATERIAL: Markers and large wall writing pad

PROCEDURE:

1. Explain to the students or group that the goal of our school is to enhance student achievement and school climate

2. Explain to the students or group that there are (2) statements on the board

3. Enhance student achievement

4. Enhance student climate

5. Ask the students what enhance means: enhance is to make things or someone better or strengthen

6. Ask the students what school climate means: school climate is the general mood or atmosphere of the school.

7. Ask the students to write down how to make a positive school climate?

8. Have the students share their answers with the class, and write their responses on the board

9. Ask the students to write bad things about when students are not on time to class

10. Ask the students what good things happen when they are on time? Is it important to you to be on time? Why? Why not?

11. Ask the students to list bad things that happen when students don't have the proper materials or attitude to learn?

12. Ask the students what good things happen when you do have the proper materials?

13. Is it important to you to be prepared? Why? Why not?

14. Ask the students how can you not be mentally prepared to learn?

15. Ask the students to list bad things that happen when students are disrespectful and rude?

16. Ask the students what good things happen when they are respectful? Is it important to you to be respectful? Why? Why not?

29. CHOOSING YOUR BEHAVIOR

OBJECTIVE: To have students understand that choosing their behavior can affect them and their school climate

MATERIAL: Markers and large wall writing pads

PROCEDURE:

1. Explain to the students that you would like their help on enhancing students achievement and school climate

2. Ask the students to write down what they would like to achieve this year at their school. In the process, sharing with the group of students

3. Ask the students how they can enhance school climate at their school

4. Tell the students that you would like for them to get into groups of 3 to 6 people.

5. Tell the students that you would like for someone to be a recorder in their group, and share the answers within the group

6. Ask the recorder to state the groups answers to the class or group without using names

7. Ask the students if they usually have the materials they need for class? Why or why not?

8. Ask the students are they prepared mentally for class? Do they have a good attitude to learn? Why or why not? Is having a good attitude to learn important? Why or why not? Write those statements down?

9. Ask the students if they are usually polite to people? Why or why not? Are you respectful to your classmates? Are you respectful to your teachers? Do you follow school rules? Why or why not?

30. LET'S DISCUSS GENDER

OBJECTIVE: Having students understand how gender criticisms can affect our- self-esteem, behavior, and body images.

MATERIAL: History texts/pictures of past and present body images of female and male

PROCEDURE:

1. This group should have 4 girls and 4 boys a total of 8 in a group the groups should be separated. Girls in one group, boys in another

2. Explain to the group that they should make a list of things that influence their self-esteem

3. After the girls present their findings, the boys will then follow-up with their findings

4. Have the group interact in an open discussion about their findings through the texts or pictures, and how it can influence self-esteem, behavior, and body images

5. Now explain to the students that they need to break up in mixed groups and discuss quietly the past, present and history through the pictures provided

6. The groups should discuss the pictures from the 1920's, 30's, 40's through the 90's

IDEA'S:

1. Have students make a collage of past and present people with different body images, however, very happy, and successful

31. BODY IMAGES THROUGH THE MEDIA

OBJECTIVE: Having the students recognize and analyze body images through the media that are unhealthy and not real

MATERIAL: Magazines

PROCEDURE:

1. Explain to the group how people in their community and about their diversity in culture, personal qualities, talents, abilities, interests, sizes and shapes

2. Explain to the group how the real people they know are different from the people they see on television and in magazines and advertising

3. Have the groups find and cut out pictures from magazines of people that look more like the real people they know.

4. Have a conversation with the group regarding their findings of real people in the magazine Did they find more pictures that were real or unrealistic of people

5. Discuss with the group how the images may affect their own body images?

6. Discuss with the group to critically analyze unrealistic body images in the media

7. Discuss with the group the photography techniques used in magazines. What is it that they create?

8. Discuss the pictures the group had cut out of the magazines of everyday people. Why are they real to them rather than the phony people?

9. Have each group continue to cut out pictures and create a collage for the classroom with the pictures they collected

IDEA's:

1. Have the group return for their next group with letters to the magazine editors regarding the unrealistic people, and images portrayed

32. ALCOHOLISM IN FAMILIES

OBJECTIVE: Having children understand how to cope with alcoholic families, and to build resiliency and develop protective coping strategies

MATERIAL: Crayons, finger paints, etc.

PROCEDURE:

1. Explain to the students that alcoholism is a disease
2. Explain that everyone gets hurt in the alcoholic family, including the children
3. Children's whose parents drink too much are not alone
4. Children do not cause parents to drink, children cannot control, or cannot cure their parents alcoholism
5. There are many ways for kids to take care of themselves when parents drink so they feel better about themselves
6. It is healing for children to express their feelings about parental drinking
7. It is ok for children to talk about parental drinking to a friend or within the safety of a group setting
8. Kids of alcoholic parents are at high risks of substance abuse themselves
9. It is important for children to reach out of the family for support
10. Discuss these parts with the children
11. Helping the children stay focused on content is less stressful, and helps prepare the children

ART ACTIVITY:

1. Hand out all crayons and finger paints to children in the group

2. Have the children in the group create a picture of their family

3. When children are finished, invite them to share their picture

4. Help children in the group as they try to present their picture. Help the children as anxiety may kick in during presentation

5. Help explore their thoughts pertaining to their family as a whole and to individual family members

6. This art activity will help any child feel comfortable expressing themselves

OTHER ART ACTIVITIES THAT HELP CHILDREN:

1. Talk about emotional reactions to living with alcoholism

2. Get an example from a child about their situation at home

3. Try to role play the situation

4. How does the situation make the children feel?

5. Puppets are a great way to role-play. Children of all ages love puppets!!

6. Puppets will help younger children process their emotional responses to alcoholism

7. This session can help resolve unexpected emotions and heighten their sense of control over future situations

MORE ART IDEA'S FOR ALCOHOLISM IN FAMILIES:

1. Other than working with puppets, everyone loves to work with

clay. Try to create the children's thought process of protection. Using the clay, allow them to freedom of expression, building protective shields. Afterwards they can paint the shields in the following session.

2. Have the children paint the shields with words

3. Have the children paint the shields with symbols

4. Have the children paint a design to show what they learned from the group to protect them from alcoholism

5. After the shields are completed, have the children present their shields

6. The presentation will help them process the skills they might have learned

7. Explain to the children they can continue to add to their shield, showing how stronger they can be

CONCLUSION:

Try to get some feedback from the children and conclude your sessions. The children do love this activity, and basically become attached, feeling protected from their new friends. Try to create an evaluation form, so they can ease out of the group process. This group activity is very powerful.

33. POSITIVE SOLUTIONS

Objective: To identify those solutions to difficult situations aren't always best or positive solutions

Materials: 5x8 index cards; crayons, pens and pencils

PROCEDURE

1. Lead your group to understand that we need to have some solution to problems or difficult situations. Talk about how solutions can help someone think positive, and satisfy their feelings. Add, that there need to be a mutual understanding between the people involved in the difficult situation.

2. Pass the index cards along to each student. Explain to the students that they would have to write down a short description of a problem or difficult situation they encountered within their family or someone they know, and the solution that came about to resolve the situation. Ask the students to write down what they would have done that would have resolved the situation in a positive way. Ask the students to not indicate their name on the cards.

3. Gather the cards and randomly distribute the cards to the students. Ask each student one at a time in the group to read the card to the group and discuss if the solution was to be positive and for the resolution to move forward.

DISCUSSION

1. Explain the solutions or positive results on each problem?

2. How convincing is each solution?

3. Have any of the positive solutions helped your thought process in resolutions?

4. After hearing other solutions, would you use them or consider using your own again?

5. What can you tell us about today's group session, and future problems?

MORE DISCUSSION

It would be a good idea to discuss that there are no one solutions to any problems. There are positive ways to help recondition negative outcomes.

34. POSITIVE CONSEQUENCES

Objective: Identifying negative problems can be a positive outcome

Materials: A picture of people who have or are dealing with problems in today's society.

A picture of athletes, drug issues, teenage crime, and suicide attempts.

PROCEDURE

1. Discuss with the students and have them express a time or place when someone they know or knew that had a problem and eventually found a positive outcome for their future. If students struggle with this thought process, help them with examples of family relationships, peer pressure, divorce, etc.

2. Have students break into groups evenly and share with them some of the photo material you have from newspapers, or magazines. Students in the group with review the pictures and discuss what might be the issues they are having.

3. Have the students discuss in group

DISCUSSION

1. Discuss how you feel about when people or you have eventually found positive outcomes from a problem?

2. Discuss what you think how many people might have took advantage of the experience from negative to positive situations have helped them?

3. Have you ever experienced a negative situation and turned it into positive?

4. How would you approach helping someone who is encountering a negative situation?

More Discussion

Discuss with the students how it is important for them to understand that they will always come across obstacles in their life, and that they need to stay strong and think positive that the negatives will turn into positives

35. TEEN MOMS TALK

OBJECTIVE: To have teenagers who are becoming new moms learn off teen mothers who are already mothers

MATERIALS: None

PROCEDURE:

1. Try to have two or three teen mothers for presentation
2. Maybe a teen mother who dropped out of school
3. Maybe a teen mother who gave her baby up for adoption
4. Explain that each teen mother will tell a story
5. Explain to the new teen moms that responsibilities are something that they need to understand
6. Explain to new teen mothers that teen moms might give out their numbers to share if there was any information they might need to get

QUESTIONS:

1. How do you feel about your decisions now? Why?
2. How do you manage school?
3. Explain why they might have dropped out of school?

CONCLUSION:

1. Having students draw a collage of their group experience
2. As students to complete a statement, "Today I learned.

36. LET'S TEXT (Popular Bonus Activity)

OBJECTIVE: In today's digital world, when is the right time to text someone? How far can we go with texting?

MATERIAL: Cell phones, I-phones, Galaxy, Blackberry, Etc. (If a student does not have a phones, he or she can be the whisperer during this activity).

PROCEDURE

The leader (Counselor) chooses a phrase statement or any message that will create a discussion of right or wrong. (Fewer than 200 words) Try to have meaning to your group and translate it to texting.

1. Be sure that all group members have each other's cell phone numbers stored in one another's cell phone memory.

2. Be sure to have students in your group circle. No student is to be out of the circle of trust. As you proceed, text your message to the first person next to you. (Try to have your message already set in your phone, so you can get started quickly).

3. The student who received the text then whispers the text message to the person sitting next to them. That person must then text the message to the person sitting next to them.

4. Continue with this process until the last person receives the message, either text or whisper.

5. Finally, when the text and whisper is completely around the circle, that last person then verbally shares the message with the group.

DISCUSSION

As the leader, you are to explain to the group some messages simply should not be communicated by electronics means. (For example: I am sorry, we cannot be together anymore). Explain to the group that more and more people are increasingly communicating through text. Is it right or wrong?

QUESTIONS:

1. WHAT DOES THE MESSAGE MEAN?
2. WHY OR WHY NOT THIS MESSAGE? (THE ONE YOUR CHOSE)
3. DID THE MESSAGE BREAKDOWN?
4. DID YOU USE BODY LANGUAGE? OR FACIAL EXPRESSIONS
5. DID BREAKDOWNS HAPPEN DURING THE WHISPER?
6. HOW DO WE SOMETIMES MIS-INTERPRET TEXT MESSAGES
7. WHAT CAN WE TAKE AWAY FROM THIS GROUP SESSION REGARDING COMMUNICATING THROUGH TEXT MESSAGING?

PART 5

SAMPLE/HELPFUL FORMS
THAT CAN BE MODIFIED

It is very important to have all your forms completed and available for your students before group or individual counseling.

Group Evaluation Form

Name of Group_____Date_____

Overall, being in this group was:

_____ helped me a lot

_____ helped me not much

_____ helped me somewhat

_____ did not help me

My feelings about this group _____
_____
_____
_____

What was most important _____
_____
_____
_____

This group helped me in _____

_____

_____

_____

This group made me improve at _____

_____

_____

_____

This group made me accomplish _____

_____

_____

_____

Parent Permission Form

FOR PARTICIPATION IN ANGER MANAGEMENT GROUP

Dear_____:

_____has been recommended to participate in an Anger Management Counseling group program that I will facilitate this year. I have met with your son/daughter and explained the content and nature of the group. This group will meet once a week. Your child is aware that he/she will miss a different class every week and he/she is responsible for obtaining make-up work from teachers. The group will be working on achieving these goals:

- Recognize the feeling of anger
- Understand the student's own anger style
- Identify what triggers the students anger
- Learn to use constructive ways to deal with anger
- Prevent inappropriate ways of dealing with anger
- Practice effective ways to manage angry feelings

Since counseling is based on trusting relationship between counselor and client, all information shared by group members is kept confidential except in certain situations in which there is an ethical responsibility to limit confidentiality. If a student reveals information about hurting himself/herself or another person, the parent will be notified.

Sincerely,

School Counselor

By signing this form, I give my informed consent for my child to participate in small group counseling. I understand that:

1. The group will provide an opportunity for members to learn and practice interpersonal skills, discuss feelings, share ideas, practice new behaviors, and make new friends

2. Anything group members share in group is completely confidential by the group leader except in the above mentioned case.

Parent Signature_____Date_____

Student Signature_____Date_____

Counseling Program

The counseling program at_____is designed to be preventive and developmental. In addition to seeing students individually and in classroom guidance, we teach skills and information in small-group settings.

Your child, _____, has expressed an interest in participating in the_____group. We emphasize to students that groups are for everyone, and participating does not indicate a problem. Groups are structured and goal focused. Students learn important life skills that enhance their ability to succeed academically and socially as well as cope with stressful situations.

Listed below are the types of groups we routinely offer.

- Student success skills: academic and social skills needed for school success
- Communication and conflict management
- You in control: self-control and anger management
- Changing family: dealing with divorce

About the Author

Rich Esposito, CAMS, M.S. is a NYS Professional School Counselor specializing in REBT in education. He is a certified specialist in Anger Management. He is certified by the National Anger Management Association (NAMA). He currently leads group-mandated clients nationally. He has worked as an adjunct professor at Mercy College teaching counseling techniques to future counselors. He works with many different cultures and religions in-group settings. He has helped many couples, and Families who have suffered loss of family in the World Trade Center attack. He maintains a private practice in anger management, and life coaching, Cortlandt Manor, New York.

In addition to being a prominent therapist, Rich has presented his work in the classroom, creating course material in "Psychology in Literature". He presented to general audiences speaking on the topics of Anger Management, depression, anxiety, bullying, and many other issues people might come across. You might have seen his published work in "Parent Magazine", "Baby Magazine" and The Bronx Times Reporter on fatherhood.

Rich is an interactive, Rational Emotive Behavior therapist in Education. He was trained by world known psychiatrist Dr. Albert Ellis using an ABC technique method. His therapeutic approach is to provide support and practical feedback to help clients effectively address personal life challenges. He integrates complementary methodologies and techniques to offer a highly personalized approach tailored to each client. With compassion and understanding, he works with each individual to help them build on their strengths and attain the personal growth they are committed to accomplishing.

CPSIA information can be obtained
at www.ICGtesting.com
Printed in the USA
FFOW01n1748121116
29320FF